P9-APW-711

PRO GAMING
FOR FORTNITERS

AN UNOFFICIAL GUIDE TO
BATTLE ROYALE

PRO GAMING FOR FORTNITERS

MASTER COMBAT SERIES BOOK #8

JASON R. RICH

Sky Pony Press
New York

Copyright © 2020 by Hollan Publishing, Inc.

Fortnite® is a registered trademark of Epic Games, Inc.

The Fortnite game is copyright © Epic Games, Inc.

Sky Pony Press books may be purchased in bulk at special discounts for sales promotion, corporate gifts, fund-raising, or educational purposes. Special editions can also be created to specifications. For details, contact the Special Sales Department, Sky Pony Press, 307 West 36th Street, 11th Floor, New York, NY 10018 or info@skyhorsepublishing.com.

Sky Pony® is a registered trademark of Skyhorse Publishing, Inc.®, a Delaware corporation.

Visit our website at www.skyhorsepublishing.com.

10 9 8 7 6 5 4 3 2 1

Library of Congress Cataloging-in-Publication Data is available on file.

Cover design by Brian Peterson
Cover artwork by Getty Images
Interior photography by Jason R. Rich

Print ISBN: 978-1-5107-5708-0
E-Book ISBN: 978-1-5107-5718-9

Printed in the United States of America

TABLE OF CONTENTS

SECTION 1

FORTNITE CONTINUES TO EVOLVE

Whether you experience this game on a Windows PC, Mac, PlayStation 4, Xbox One, Nintendo Switch, Nintendo Switch Lite, iPhone, iPad, Android-based mobile device, or one of the newest generation of console-based systems, the excitement and challenges associated with participating in a Fortnite: Battle Royale *Solo, Duos,* or *Squads* match are unparalleled in the gaming world.

If you're like the more than 250 million gamers from around the world, for up to or more than 10 gaming seasons, you've been working hard to master your overall *Fortnite: Battle Royale* gaming skills.

Not everyone has what it takes to have their soldier leap from the Battle Bus and drop down to the mysterious island, only to be confronted with up to 99 adversaries (each controlled in real time by another gamer) who are all simultaneously trying to achieve #1 Victory Royale.

You may think that ranking within the top 5 during a match is impressive (which in many ways it is), but the true winners are those sole survivors who outsmart, out fight, out build, out maneuver, and ultimately eliminate all of their adversaries. At the end of a match, there's only one true winner. Whether you're experiencing the match alone, with a partner, as part of a four-person squad, or as a member of a team, becoming that sole survivor is always the true objective!

A Pro Gamer's Objectives

Only the world's most elite gamers have achieved all of these objectives and can proudly call themselves a "pro gamer." For the rest of us, countless hours of practice and hard work lie ahead trying to achieve the following objectives:

- Learning all about the ever-changing arsenal of weapons available during matches and knowing exactly how to utilize them in combat situations.
- Discovering how to best utilize the vehicles and transportation options made available for getting your soldier safely around the island.
- Finding the best ways to find and gather ammo, loot, and items during each visit to the island.
- Mastering the speed and "art" of building.
- Memorizing all of the points of interest on the constantly evolving map.
- Developing your muscle memory associated with maneuvering your soldier, aiming weapons, building, and surviving during each match.
- Collecting a lit assortment of outfits and related bling to customize the appearance of your soldier.
- Figuring out how to outmaneuver the deadly storm.
- Determining the best ways to analyze and defeat the enemy soldiers you encounter on the island.
- Perfecting your survival skills, so you're able to keep your soldier healthy and strong during matches.
- Uncovering the best strategies to implement so your soldier consistently makes it into the End Game (the final few minutes of a match when only a few soldiers remain alive, and the storm continues to close in).
- Being able to repeatedly experience the thrill of achieving #1 Victory Royale.
- Participating and ranking in the official *Fortnite: Battle Royale* Events hosted within the game by Epic Games. From the Lobby screen, select the Compete tab to view current and upcoming Events. Ranking highly or winning daily and weekly Events (sometimes referred to as Cups) could earn you a spot in higher-level competitions that lead up to the annual *Fortnite* World Cup.

Only after you've managed to achieve all of these objectives, and perhaps a few others, can you begin to consider referring to yourself as a "pro level" *Fortnite: Battle Royale* gamer. For many people, however, a few or perhaps all of these objectives are yet to be achieved.

All that you have experienced to date playing this incredibly popular game has led to one thing—preparing yourself for what Epic Games refers to as Fortnite: Battle Royale *Chapter 2.*

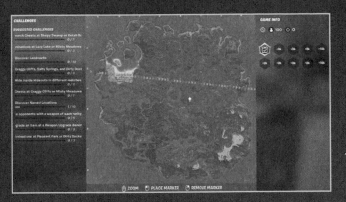
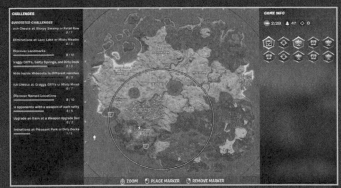

One of your first objectives when playing Fortnite: Battle Royale Chapter 2 is to reveal the entire island map, one region or point of interest at a time.

All of the same skills and game-related muscle memory you've already worked so hard to acquire must now be put to the ultimate test as you experience an entirely redesigned island that's filled with all new points of interest; updated weapons, loot items, tools, and vehicles; and countless new types of challenges offered by the game itself and the other gamers you continue to face during each match experienced on the mysterious island. While you'll be introduced to many new things on the island during each new gaming season, some things, like Ziplines, continue to provide soldiers with a quick and easy way to get around parts of the island.

When it comes to mastering Fortnite: Battle Royale, if there's one thing you can count on, it's that the game continues to evolve! Just about every week, Epic Games releases an update (referred to as a "patch") that introduces something new into the game, or somehow alters various aspects of the game you may already be familiar with. What this means is that as a gamer, you must continue perfecting your gaming skills while learning how to adapt everything you know about playing Fortnite: Battle Royale to address the new challenges you're confronted with during each match.

The most accomplished *Fortnite: Battle Royale* gamers from around the world take a multi-faceted approach to achieve ongoing success. It all starts with becoming well acquainted with every aspect and nuance of the game itself. This includes mastering your combat, survival, exploration, and building skills, which takes practice . . . a lot of practice!

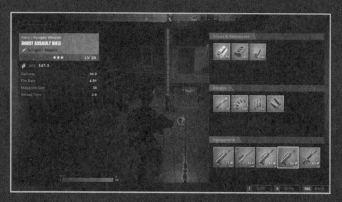

With new weapons and items constantly being introduced into the game, one of your core responsibilities is to collect and manage the most powerful arsenal possible, and to make sure you have plenty of ammo on hand for the various weapons you possess. Shown here is the soldier's Backpack Inventory screen, from which you can manage your soldier's arsenal, ammo, items, and the tools they have on hand.

Using the items you find and collect, such as this Shield Potion or Bandages, you'll need to keep your soldier's Health and Shield meters at their highest possible levels to help ensure survival.

Some things in Fortnite: Battle Royale *always remain the same. For example, finding and opening Chests, Supply Drops, and Loot Llamas will always provide a nice selection of weapons, ammo, and loot for your soldier, assuming you're able to approach and open these items safely. Meanwhile, Ammo Boxes continue to be a superb source for collecting ammunition for your soldier's weapons. Ammo Boxes are typically a great source for Rockets (as well as the four other ammo types).*

One new tool added at the start of Chapter 2 was Fishing Rods. These can be used within most bodies of water to collect fish, but also acquire random weapons and items from within a lake or stream that can be added to your soldier's inventory. Only take time for fishing if you know the area is clear of enemies. If someone launches a surprise attack, chances are you'll be out in the open while holding a fishing rod (unless you build a structure around your soldier). It takes a few valuable seconds to switch from the fishing rod being your soldier's active tool to selecting and using a weapon that's stored in one of the soldier's other inventory slots.

The deadly storm continues to be a huge threat as you explore the island. As the storm expands and moves, it drives all of the surviving soldiers closer and closer together, until those who remain during the End Game (the final few minutes of a match) are forced to fight for their survival.

What It Takes to Become a Pro *Fortnite: Battle Royale* Gamer

Okay, so you may be wondering what it takes to become a pro *Fortnite: Battle Royale* gamer. The truth is, this varies somewhat, depending on how competitive you want to be, and how aggressive you are when it comes to achieving a high ranking in official competitions and on the game's Leaderboards.

Step #1 is to become a really awesome and well-rounded *Fortnite: Battle Royale* gamer, regardless of which gaming season you're experiencing.

Step #2 is to give yourself every possible competitive edge by upgrading your gaming gear.

Step #3 is to practice and fine-tune your muscle memory associated with *Fortnite: Battle Royale.* This means that without having to think about it, your brain knows which keyboard or controller button(s) to press in order to quickly move your soldier around on the island, select a weapon, accurately aim/reload the active weapon, fire the active weapon, take evasive actions when necessary, be able to build at lightning-fast speed, keep your soldier healthy, manage your soldier's inventory, and be able to perfectly adapt and/or execute whatever strategies you deem necessary to achieve your immediate in-game objectives.

Step #4 requires you to continuously work your way through a Battle Pass and complete each of its objectives and 100 Tiers during each and every gaming season.

Step #5 requires you to consistently be able to achieve #1 Victory Royale during whichever types of matches you participate in, while at the same time, successfully completing Challenges, and ranking in (or winning) officially sanctioned competitions offered within the game when you select the Compete tab at the top of the Lobby screen.

Step #6 often involves you expanding your *Fortnite* career to become not just a successful competitive gamer, but perhaps a member of Epic Games' Support-A-Creator program, and/or a popular *Fortnite: Battle Royale* streamer on YouTube, Mixer, or Twitch.

Once you build a following of at least 1,000 followers on a popular social media platform, you can apply to join Epic Game's Support-A-Creator program. Then, when your fans and followers opt to support you while they play Fortnite, you'll receive $5.00 (US) for every 10,000 V-Bucks they spend within the game.

Once you're approved for the Support-A-Creator program, you're able to publish and promote your own Fortnite: Creative maps, like this mini Deathrun course. Enter Map Code 7600-2201-3273 to experience it.

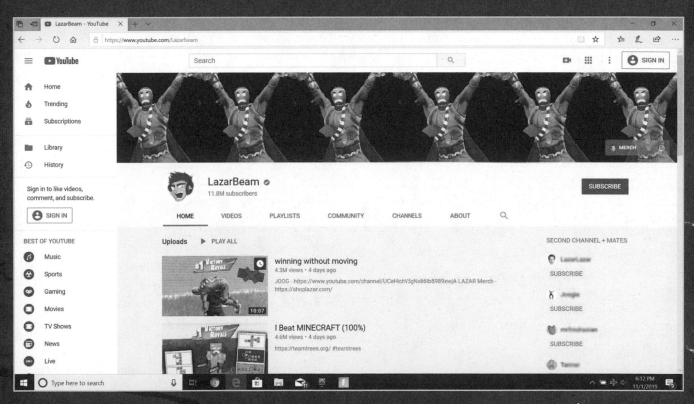

Building up an audience in the thousands or even millions, and then earning revenue from your live streams and videos, from paid sponsorships, and from competition wins have become viable money-making opportunities for countless gamers. Check out LazarBeam's YouTube channel (www.youtube.com/Lazarbeam), for example. He's a mega-popular Fortnite gamer from Australia with around 12 million YouTube channel subscribers.

Step #7 involves being recruited onto a competitive team/eSports organization, such as TSM (Team MoloMid), FaZe Clan, Ghost Gaming, Team Liquid, NRG eSports, Team Secret, 100 Thieves, Fnatc, Solary, or OpTic Gaming.

Learn About Your Favorite *Fortnite* Role Models

If you want to follow in the footsteps of some of the best-of-the-best *Fortnite* gamers and social media influencers, be sure to check out these 25 pros (listed in alphabetical order, not by accomplishment), and consider modeling your gaming career after any of them.

25 World Famous Professional *Fortnite* Gamers

To learn more about each of these gamers (and others like them), enter their names into any search engine (such as Google, Yahoo!, or Bing), or use the Search tool built into a popular game streaming or social media service.

1. **Ceeday**
2. **CouRangeJD**
3. **Daequan**
4. **Dakotaz**
5. **DrDisrespect**
6. **DrLupo**
7. **Faze Cloakzy**
8. **FaZe TFue**
9. **Hamlinz**
10. **HS2 Delirious**
11. **KingRichard**
12. **Kyle Giersdorf (winner of the 2019 *Fortnite* World Cup)**
13. **LazarBeam**
14. **Maximilianmus**
15. **Muselk**
16. **Nick Eh 30**
17. **Nickmercs**
18. **Nickmercs**
19. **Ninja**
20. **Nyhrox**
21. **SypherPK**
22. **Tfue**
23. **TimTheTatman**
24. **TSM_Daequan**
25. **TSM_Myth**

Also, be sure to check out some of the many independent *Fortnite*-related websites that offer up-to-date player rankings, along with details about each gamer's gear. Some of these sites include:

- **Fortbase.net**—https://fortbase.net/leadboards
- **Fortnite Stats**—https://fortnitestats.net
- **Fortnite Stats & Leaderboards**—https://fortnitestats.com
- **Fortnite Tracker Network (TRN)**—https://fortnitetracker.com/leaderboards
- **OP.GG Fortnite**—https://fortnite.op.gg
- **Ranker**—www.ranker.com/list/best-professional-fortnite-players/ranker-games
- **Storm Shield**—www.stormshield.one

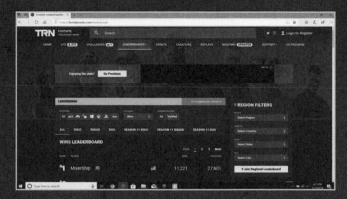

From the Fortnite *Tracker Network* website, it's possible to see the stats of almost any Fortnite gamer, including your favorite pros.

By visiting the Storm Shield website, you're able to access Leaderboards based on game type (Solo, Duos, or Squads), gaming platform (PC, PlayStation 4, or Xbox One), or Metrics (score, wins, Top 10/5/3, Top 25/12/6, Kills, Win Percentage, etc.).

Check out Ninja's profile on Fortbase.net. In addition to his player stats, this website shows his gaming equipment, as well as his customized video settings, controller settings, and key binds.

Top-scoring gamers and top-ranked gamers also appear on the Leaderboards that are offered within the Fortnite: Battle Royale game. To access this ever-changing information, from the Lobby, select the Career tab (displayed near the top-center of the screen), and then select the Profile option. Next, choose the Leaderboard type by selecting one of the tabs displayed near the top-center of the screen. These include: Score, Placed Top 25, Placed Top 10, and Global Wins.

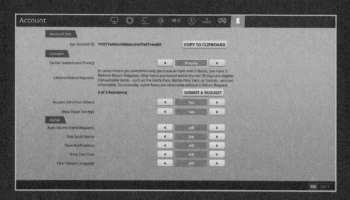

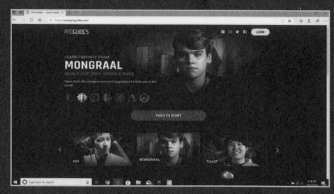

Until you get really good, to avoid having the public (random gamers) be able to see your gaming stats, consider making this information private. To do this, access the Settings menu, select the Account option, and set the Career Leaderboard Privacy option to Private.

A growing number of online services allow gamers to hire experienced Fortnite coaches by the hour. If you have the skill and experience to become a professional coach, you could potentially be hired by one of these companies and then make some extra money by sharing your Fortnite skills with newbs, for example.

You might also consider becoming a professional *Fortnite* coach (or hiring a coach for yourself to help you improve one or more aspects of your gaming technique or skillset). Even some of the world's highest-ranked *Fortnite* gamers are "trained" by professional coaches. As a result, numerous independent coaching services have been established, including:

Some coaches who charge by the hour will help you become a better gamer, while others are a bit sketchy and may not help you achieve the results you desire, so proceed with caution when hiring and paying for a coach to help you.

- **CoachingGames.net**—https://coaching-games.net/coaching/fortnite-coaching
- **Gamer Sensei**—www.gamersensei.com/games/fortnite-coaching
- **GamingCoach.gg**—https://gamingcoach.gg/game/fortnite
- **ProBoosting**—www.proboosting.net/fortnite-coaching
- **ProGuides**—www.proguides.com

If your goal is to become a professional coach, be sure to team up with a reputable coaching organization, such as InstaPro by ProGuides.

Discover Your Own Gaming Style, But Don't Be Predictable!

Over time, most *Fortnite: Battle Royale* gamers develop their own personal gaming style. Perhaps you'll discover specific points of interest on the map that you get to know extra well and prefer to fight within. Maybe you'll discover you're better at long-range combat, as opposed to close-range combat within buildings or structures, for example.

With experience, you might determine that you prefer to jump right into the combat action at the start of each match, with the goal of achieving as many eliminations as possible, as opposed to taking your time early on during a match to first build up your soldier's arsenal, before seeking out combat situations.

Some gamers select one or two favorite weapons that they're able to utilize with the best speed and accuracy, or they develop an extra proficiency at building, for example. Others opt to fully utilize vehicles to get around the island, while some prefer other modes of transportation that they believe give their soldier an edge.

While working toward becoming a pro gamer, analyze your own gaming habits, likes, and dislikes. Begin to formulate your own, unique gaming style. However, as you begin to achieve success using that style or collection of strategies, don't rely on those habits exclusively. When you do this, your competition will be able to more easily predict what you'll do next and how you'll handle specific situations. Acting predictably on the island is a huge mistake!

Getting to know your adversaries and how they'll likely react, however, gives you a tremendous strategic advantage. This makes it easier to pinpoint and exploit your competition's weaknesses. As you study your enemies during matches, look for patterns in their behavior, strategies, and actions. Do they rely heavily on a specific weapon, item, or maneuver? Determine when and where they're able to achieve the greatest accuracy and threat to your soldier, and in what situations those same gamers tend to show weakness, a lack of speed, or poor coordination.

Anytime you're able to identify a weakness in your adversary, exploit it! For example, if you see an enemy relying heavily on a specific weapon or repeating the same attack maneuvers over and over during a match, choose a weapon that's more powerful, offers better accuracy, or that will force the adversary to break their pattern. Get them out of their comfort zone and force them to think fast and react even faster as they're pushed into improvising and abandoning their planned strategy. This will often cause them to lose focus, panic, or make mistakes.

At the same time, while you're relying on specific weapons, items, and/or offensive or defensive maneuvers to achieve your own success, avoid following patterns. In other words, be unpredictable!

When your opponents can't figure out what you'll do next, they won't be able to pre-plan counter strategies or implement well-thought-out defenses. Keep your opponents on their toes and guessing. If you lead them to believe you're about to do one thing, trick them by doing something vastly different at the last moment. This will likely confuse your enemies and give you an edge.

You'll quickly discover that speed, decisiveness, and unpredictability are three keys to winning most matches, especially when you know the terrain you're fighting in, you've amassed a powerful arsenal, and you're comfortable building when and where it's necessary.

Section 3—Fine-Tune Your Fortnite: Battle Royale *Gaming Skills* will help you define your own gaming style, identify and overcome your weaknesses as a gamer, and help you identify combat scenarios and terrain types where you're most apt to succeed based on your skill level and experience.

What This Unofficial Guide Offers

This is the eighth book in the mega-popular, unofficial *Master Combat Series*. Each book in this series focuses on one or more specific aspects of successfully playing *Fortnite: Battle Royale.* As you're about to discover, this guide is jam-packed with tips and strategies that'll help you up your game when it comes to playing *Fortnite: Battle Royale*, especially if your goal is to ultimately achieve "pro" status as a gamer.

Each section of this guide covers vital information you'll need to become a pro. For example,

Section 2—Upgrade Your Gaming Gear to Pro Level focuses on choosing the best gaming system, controllers, keyboard, mouse, gaming headset, and related gear to help improve your speed and reaction time when playing *Fortnite: Battle Royale*, keeping in mind that a millisecond can mean the difference between survival and defeat during an intense combat situation.

In *Section 3—Fine-Tune Your* Fortnite: Battle Royale *Gaming Skills,* the focus is on improving your core gaming skills, including: building up and managing your arsenal; improving your aim and targeting accuracy; mastering the art of combat strategy formulation; rounding out your building skills; keeping your soldier strong during matches; improving your exploration skills; and perfecting your offensive and defensive fighting techniques.

Once you've become a really good gamer, *Section 4—How to Take Your Gaming to the Pro Level,* discusses many of the ways you can pursue a "career" as a pro gamer, whether you choose to compete for prize money or pursue other money-making opportunities available to highly skilled *Fortnite* gamers. You'll learn what your options are and how to pursue them from this section.

When you're ready to showcase your skills online, *Section 5—How to Become a* Fortnite: Battle Royale Streamer *and Build an Audience* teaches you how to record and publish *Fortnite*-related videos on social media (such as YouTube), plus explains how to stream live on services like Twitch, Mixer, and YouTube. You'll discover what it takes to build a massive audience and become a social media influencer in the gaming world.

Finally, *Section 6—Fortnite: Battle Royale Online Resources* is chock full of useful online resources related to all aspects of *Fortnite*. Discover the best sites for staying up-to-date on the latest *Fortnite*-related news, including competitions.

Expect Evolution!

While the island map, weapon selection, vehicles, items, the behavior of the deadly storm, the selection of soldier outfits and emotes, the game play modes offered within the game, and the challenges you face on the island will continuously change, many of the core combat, survival, and building strategies you'll need to master remain pretty consistent from gaming season to gaming season.

Power boats capable of shooting projectile weapons, Fishing Rods, and the ability for a soldier to swim (quickly) when submerged in water were among the new additions added to Chapter 2, Season 1.

During your soldier's freefall at the start of a match, check out the graphic altimeter that's now displayed to the immediate left of the mini-map (located in the top-right corner of the game screen on most gaming systems).

Helping you understand the core elements of *Fortnite: Battle Royale* will make you a better gamer, and it's a main focus of what you'll find within the unofficial guides that are part of this *Master Combat Series*. Thus, while this book was created during *Fortnite: Battle Royale's* Chapter 2, Season 1, much of what you'll learn throughout this guide applies to *all* gaming seasons.

After reading this guide, you'll likely need to get yourself up to date on the latest selection of weapons, ammo, vehicles, items, and map points of interest currently featured within the game, but you'll already have learned important core strategies related to combat, survival, exploration, and building, for example, plus understand what it'll take to advance your gaming skills to the "pro" level.

To learn about other books in the unofficial *Master Combat Series* by author Jason R. Rich, be sure to visit **www.FortniteGameBooks.com**.

One of the best ways to stay informed when it comes to *Fortnite*-related news is to check out the News section within the game itself.

From the Lobby, click on the Menu icon displayed in the top-right corner of the screen (on most gaming systems). This icon looks like three horizontal lines. Next, select the News option.

*Check out the official Fortnite website from Epic Games by pointing your favorite web browser to: **www.epicgames.com/fortnite/en-US/news**.*

You'll also discover that the folks at Epic Games (the creators of Fortnite) are very active on YouTube (www.youtube.com/user/epicfortnite/featured), Facebook (www.facebook.com/FortniteGame), Twitter (https://twitter.com/FortniteGame), Twitch (www.twitch.tv/fortnite), and Discord (https://discordapp.com/invite/fortnite). Within Section 6—Fortnite: Battle Royale Online Resources, you'll find a comprehensive listing of independent online resources to help you stay up to date on all things Fortnite-related.

For now, however, get started by installing *Fortnite: Battle Royale* for free onto your computer or console-based system, and then

enhance your experience by purchasing the current season's Battle Pass. Each Battle Pass requires you to complete challenges and objectives designed to round out and improve your gaming skills.

Acquire the Current Season's Battle Pass

To purchase the basic Battle Pass for the current gaming season, from the Lobby, select the Battle Pass tab displayed near the top-center of the screen, and then choose the Buy Battle Pass option.

The cost of a basic, 100-Tier, seasonal Battle Pass is 950 V-Bucks (approximately $9.50 US). Shown here is the purchase screen for the Chapter 2, Season 1 Battle Pass.

You can also upgrade the basic Battle Pass by purchasing the season's Battle Bundle for 2,800 V-Bucks (approximately $28.00 US). This allows you to instantly unlock 25 Tiers within the current Battle Pass, which includes several awesome and exclusive soldier outfits, accessories, and emotes (all of which are for cosmetic purposes only and do not impact a soldier's in-game strength, capabilities, or speed).

Prior to purchasing a Battle Pass, from the Battle Pass screen, click on the View Battle Pass Details button to see the rewards associated with each Tier of the current season's Battle Pass. Keep in mind, at the end of each gaming season, the current Battle Pass expires and a new one can be purchased at the start of the following gaming season. A typical season lasts between three and four months.

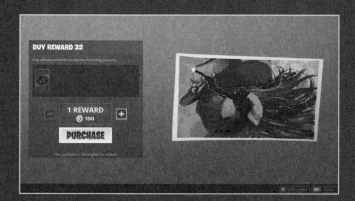

If you don't want to complete the required objectives and challenges to work your way through each Tier of a Battle Pass, you always have the option to spend 150 V-Bucks (about $1.50) to immediately unlock individual Tiers and instantly receive the reward associated with that Tier.

Once a Battle Pass has been acquired, its Tiers and related rewards are displayed along the bottom of the screen. Battle Pass rewards include exclusive outfits, various types of emotes (including dance moves), loading screen graphics, 100 V-Buck bundles, wraps, harvesting tool designs, glider designs, music tracks, outfit styles, contrail designs, back bling designs, and other exclusive cosmetic items that are not available elsewhere.

Purchasing a Battle Pass is always optional, but only by purchasing a Battle Pass can you unlock the exclusive and limited-time outfits and rewards associated with each Battle Pass Tier. Once a Battle Pass ends, these rewards are no longer offered. If you manage to unlock all of the Battle Pass rewards, the collective value of them far exceeds the number of V-Bucks spent to purchase the Battle Pass or Battle Bundle.

More Ways to Customize Your Soldier's Appearance

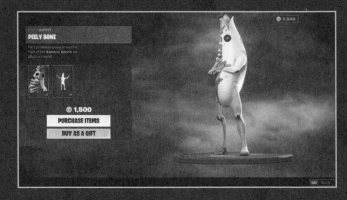

Shown here is the Epic-ranked Peely Bone Outfit, which is part of the Banana Bunch set. As you can see, it's priced at 1,500 V-Bucks (about $15.00 US) and it includes an exclusive emote.

From the Item Shop, a different selection of soldier outfits and related accessories (including back bling designs, harvesting tool designs, glider designs, and emotes) continue to be made available each day. From the Lobby, select the Item Shop option to see what's currently being offered.

To make purchases within the Item Shop, you'll need to acquire or purchase V-Bucks using real money. To do this, from the Lobby, click on the Store tab. Several different V-Buck bundles are sold separately. For example, 1,000 V-Bucks are priced at $9.99 (US), while 2,800 V-Bucks will cost you $24.99 (US). If you want to purchase 5,000 V-Bucks at once and save some money, you can do this for $39.99 (US). A 13,500 bundle of V-bucks is priced at $99.99 (US).

In addition, throughout each gaming season, Epic Games will periodically offer a limited-time "Pack," which includes one or more exclusive outfits and items for between $4.99 and $17.99. These are only available from the Store, not the Item Shop. Once these offers expire, they are no longer available, so if you're looking to collect truly exclusive and limited edition outfits, accessory items, and emotes, for example, you'll definitely want to unlock what's offered as Battle Pass rewards, plus purchase special "Packs" offered from the Shop.

design, harvesting tool design, glider design, outfit style, contrail design, weapon/item/vehicle wrap(s), and emotes of their choice—allowing their soldier to stand out from the crowd and be instantly recognizable.

You can then round out your collection of Locker items by purchasing outfits and items from the Item Shop and/or by completing other in-game Challenges that allows you to unlock special items, such as unique outfit styles. When an outfit or item is ranked "Legendary," this means it's rare, and typically won't be reintroduced into the game anytime soon. These also tend to be the most expensive items if they're being purchased from the Item Shop.

While most gamers love to be able to customize the appearance of their soldier during matches, many pro gamers are known for having their favorite Legendary outfit(s), which they then customize with a back bling

As always, it's from the game mode selection menu that you're able to choose between participating in a Solo, Duos, Squads, Team Rumble, Arena, or another limited-time game play mode. You're also able to access Fortnite: Creative *and Playground mode from this menu.*

SECTION 2

UPGRADE YOUR GAMING GEAR TO PRO LEVEL

When it comes to truly becoming a *Fortnite: Battle Royale* master—someone who can literally crush their competition during every match—you'll need more than just top-notch gaming skills. Speed is also an essential component to victory!

Your ability to quickly and precisely navigate your soldier around the island, both on foot and when riding or driving in some type of vehicle, is an absolute necessity. This includes having the wherewithal to take cover when needed, and then hastily go on the offensive anytime an attack needs to be launched.

Other core gaming skills that require speed include building and repairing structures (the ability to quickly switch between Combat and Building mode), quickly using items to replenish your soldier's Health and Shield meters, or switching between the main game screen and your soldier's Backpack Inventory screen, for example.

Equally, if not more important, is your ability to quickly and accurately aim, shoot, and reload weapons, and then take cover during incoming attacks.

During any *Fortnite: Battle Royale* match, milliseconds matter! Even the slightest hesitation or delay on your part could be disastrous. As a gamer, knowing exactly which controller or keyboard/mouse button to press and when requires a lot of practice, so you're able to develop your game-specific muscle memory.

Maximize Your Internet Connection Speed

To further improve your reaction time and overall speed, consider your Internet connection. You'll almost always achieve a faster and more reliable connection if your computer or gaming console is connected directly to the modem or router using an Ethernet cable, as opposed to relying on a wireless (Wi-Fi) connection.

In other words, consider connecting an Ethernet cable between your computer or gaming console (PS4, Xbox One, or Nintendo Switch, for example) and your Internet's modem or router.

Virtually all computers have a built-in Ethernet port, or a low cost Ethernet to USB (USB-C) adapter that allows for a direct (cable) connection to your modem or router. Establishing a direct Internet connection should improve your connection speed and overall game performance in terms of response time.

Both the PlayStation 4 and Xbox One, as well as most other new console-based gaming systems have a built in Ethernet port. All you need is an appropriate length Ethernet cable (sold separately) to connect between the back of the console and your modem or router. Ethernet cables come in lengths between 3 and 25 feet and are sold at computer and consumer electronics stores. They tend to be less expensive if you shop for them online from Amazon.com or eBay.com, for example.

To directly connect the Nintendo Switch to your modem/router, you'll need to use the system's dock, and purchase the optional Nintendo Switch Wired Internet LAN Adapter ($29.99) from Nintendo.

When gaming on a mobile device, such as an iPhone or iPad, a Wi-Fi Internet connection is typically faster than a 3G, 4G LTE, or 5G-E cellular data connection. However, when true 5G cellular data service is introduced in 2020 or beyond, this will likely provide a superior connection to the Internet that's best suited when playing *Fortnite: Battle Royale* while on the go.

If you consistently notice significant game lags or glitches with your Internet connection when playing *Fortnite: Battle Royale*, it may be necessary to contact your Internet Service Provider (ISP) to upgrade your modem, router, and/or available connection speed.

From your computer's web browser, to test your Internet connection speed, visit a free website, such as www.Fast.com or www.speedtest.net.

Working with In-Game Settings

The next step related to improving speed and response time when playing *Fortnite: Battle Royale* is to tinker with the options available from the game's Settings menu. How you adjust the game's settings should be based on your Internet connection speed, your gaming hardware, as well as your skills and experience as a gamer.

In other words, don't just copy the game settings used by a pro gamer and think doing this will help you. In most cases, it won't. In fact, simply copying another gamer's settings could be detrimental since these were adjusted based on their own equipment, gaming style, and personal preferences.

To improve your reaction time and accuracy when it comes to in-game movement and aiming, for example, in between matches, access the Settings menu from the Lobby. To do this, click on the Game Menu icon that's displayed in the top-right corner of the screen. This icon looks like three horizontal lines.

From the Game Menu, select the Settings option.

Fortnite: Battle Royale's Settings menu is divided up into several submenus, each with its own tab that's displayed near the top-center of the screen. On a Windows PC, for example, these submenu tabs include: Video, Game, Controller Sensitivity, Brightness, Audio, Accessibility, Input, Controller, and Account.

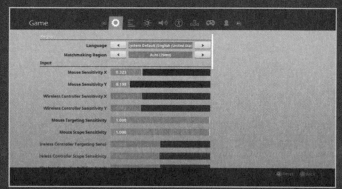

On console-based gaming systems, such as the PlayStation 4 (shown here), the Settings submenu tabs include: Game, Controller Sensitivity, Brightness, Audio, Accessibility, Input (only if a keyboard and mouse is connected), Wireless Controller, and Account.

As you're experimenting to discover the best settings for your gaming hardware, only make small, incremental changes to one or two options at a time, and then play a match or two to see the impact your changes made to the game's performance, reaction time, your aiming accuracy, and your overall speed, for example. Later, make additional changes as needed.

Adjusting the Video Submenu Options

Available exclusively within the Windows PC and Mac versions of *Fortnite: Battle Royale*, the Video submenu within Settings is used to tweak the game based on your gaming hardware. The main considerations here are the overall processing speed and capabilities of your computer and graphics card. If you're using an older, slow computer, to maximize your computer's performance, you'll likely need to tinker with the options available from this menu.

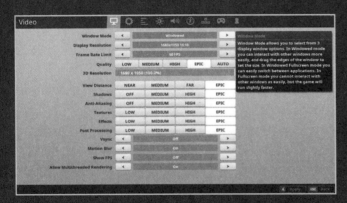

Assuming you have a relatively "modern" computer, set the Quality setting to Epic or Auto, and the 3D Resolution option to the highest level possible, unless choosing a higher option negatively impacts game play.

Again, based on the computer and graphics card's speed, processing power, and overall capabilities, you may improve your gaming experience if you adjust the Window Mode option from Full Screen to Windowed Full Screen or Windowed, for example.

More importantly, however, the Display Resolution and Frame Rate Limit will directly impact the game's performance. Choose the highest resolution your equipment is capable of, but that doesn't cause lags or glitches during game play. Finding the ideal settings might require some experimentation on your part. Lowering the Resolution and/or Frame Rate will improve overall performance but decrease the quality and detail of the graphics you see during the game.

For View Distance, Shadows, Anti-Aliasing, Textures, Effects, and Post Processing, choosing one of the options other than Epic will reduce the quality of the graphics you see and experience during the game, but will likely improve the performance and speed (and help you avoid glitches or lags). Ideally, you want to set each of these options to Epic, assuming your computer's processor and graphics card can handle it.

Based on the power and capabilities of your computer, it might become necessary to upgrade your computer, or at least its graphics card and memory, to achieve the best possible performance and avoid having your gaming hardware hinder your gaming experience or reaction time in any way.

According to Epic Games, the <u>minimum</u> computer hardware requirements for *Fortnite: Battle Royale* (Chapter 2 or later) include:

Video Card	Intel HD 4000 on PC or Intel Iris Pro 5200 on Mac
Processor	Core i3 2.4Ghz
Memory	4 GB RAM
Operating System	Windows 7/8/10 64-bit or macOS High Sierra (10.13.6+)

To experience the best possible game play experience, however, Epic Games recommends these hardware requirements for *Fortnite: Battle Royale* (Chapter 2 or later):

Video Card	NVIDIA GeForce GTX 660 or AMD Radeon HD 7870 or equivalent DX11 GPU
Video Memory	2 GB VRAM
Processor	Core i5 2.8 Ghz
Memory	8 GB RAM
OS	Windows 7/8/10 64-bit or macOS Mojave (10.14.4+)

Keep in mind, all of the console-based gaming systems have the computing and graphics power needed to experience *Fortnite: Battle Royale* without requiring upgrades or modification. If you're playing on a PS4, XBox One, or a more recently released console-based system, you can improve your gaming experience by upgrading your wireless controller. If you're storing a lot of games and game-related data within your system's hard drive, you might also consider upgrading the hard drive with one that has a larger capacity, as well as a faster read/write speed.

Adjusting the Game Submenu Options

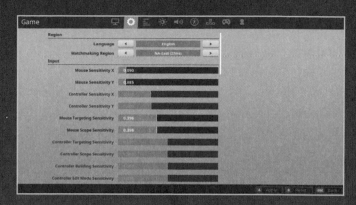

To improve your reaction time and accuracy when playing Fortnite: Battle Royale, adjusting the options available from the Game submenu will likely be beneficial. How you adjust these options should be based on your gaming hardware, skill/ experience level as a gamer, and your personal preference.

Tweak the options that enhance your game play experience by improving your reaction time and accuracy when it comes to navigating around within the game, aiming/shooting weapons, and building, for example.

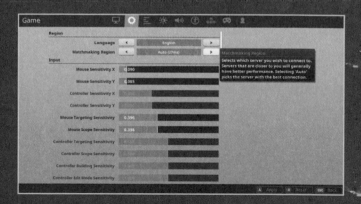

To experience the fastest Internet connection between your equipment and the Epic Games servers, for the Matchmaking Region option, choose Auto. Next to each option you'll see a number in parentheses. This indicates the current connection speed possible, based on your location..The higher the speed, the better.

You'll typically experience the best connection speed between your gaming equipment and the Epic Games servers if you're linking with a server that's located in your geographic region. This means that when the game matches you up with opponents, or teams you up with a partner or squad mates, these random matchups will be with people in your geographic region.

To experience the game with players from other regions, you can manually switch the Matchmaking Region option to North America (NA) East, North America (NA) West, Europe, Oceania, Brazil, Asia, or Middle East. In most cases, however, choosing a region that's not your own will slow down the connection and could result in lags or glitches when playing *Fortnite: Battle Royale*.

Below the Input heading within the Game submenu, you'll discover a selection of options for adjusting the Mouse and/or Controller Sensitivity for handling in-game tasks like movement, targeting weapons, targeting scoped weapons, building, and editing building tiles. Adjusting these options will impact the sensitivity of your mouse or controller. Each option should be adjusted based on your personal preferences.

Again, when adjusting various Sensitivity options, make small tweaks to relevant settings, and then play a match or two to determine the impact those changes have on game play. Over time, make additional tweaks as needed.

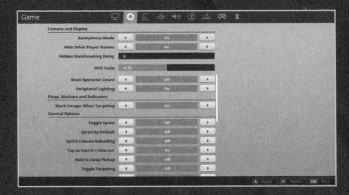

Below the Camera and Display heading are a selection of options that allow you to customize what information is displayed on the game screens at any given time during matches. For example, to reduce on-screen clutter, you could adjust the HUD (Heads Up Display) Scale option to reduce the size of information displayed on the screen.

Shown here, the HUD Scale option has been reduced to 0.25. Notice that game-related information and icons on the screen now appear much smaller. In fact, they're hardly visible.

Shown here is the HUD Scale at the default 0.75 level.

Shown here is the HUD Scale at the default 1.0 level. Notice all of the information displayed on the screen, such as the mini-map and the soldier's inventory, are displayed much larger.

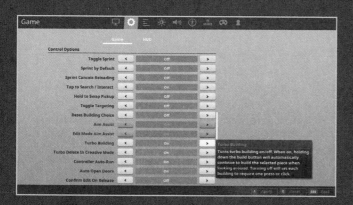

Scroll down within the Game submenu to the Control Options heading. Here you'll discover almost 20 different options that allow you to alter how you interact within the game. Some of these options, such as Aim Assist, Edit Mode Assist, Controller Auto-Run, Auto Open Doors, and Auto Pick Up Item will make it easier to interact with the game since fewer keyboard or controller button pushes will be required to handle common tasks.

Adjusting the Controller Sensitivity Submenu Options

This settings-related submenu was added in conjunction with Fortnite: Battle Royale Chapter 2, Season 1. It allows you to customize how your handheld controller (as opposed to a mouse/keyboard) handles looking around, building, and editing buildings.

The Look Sensitivity option allows you to adjust how quickly your view within the game rotates. There are 10 incremental options to choose from, with the default option being 4 (Normal). When you increase this sensitivity, the view rotation speed increases. When you decrease this sensitivity, the view rotation speed decreases. The same is true for the Aim Sensitivity option.

The Build Mode Sensitivity Multiplier and Edit Mode Sensitivity Multiplier relates to your viewing rotation speed when in Building mode and using a controller. You have the ability to increase or decrease these viewing rotation speeds.

If you turn on the Use Advanced Options feature, an extensive submenu will be displayed along with a warning message. Keep in mind, any significant changes made to these options could negatively impact your aiming speed and accuracy.

Proceed with caution when adjusting any of the Advanced—Look Sensitivity or Advanced—Aim Down Sights (ADS) Sensitivity options. Only make small changes, test the impact those changes have on the game and your controller, and then make additional tweaks as needed.

Adjusting the Input Submenu Options

If you'll be controlling Fortnite: Battle Royale *using a mouse/keyboard combination (as opposed to a controller), the options available from the Input submenu allow you to customize the key bindings associated with every action or function you'll control within the game.*

At their default settings, the key bindings are designed to give you easy access to the most commonly used features and functions within the game, with related features and functions often operated using keyboard keys that are close to each other. Many of these default key bindings are similar to what's used when playing other "battle royale" style games, which makes memorizing the keyboard and mouse functionality that much easier.

Based on your gaming style and personal preferences, you're able to reassign any keyboard key and/or mouse button to perform any other in-game function or task. As you scroll down this menu, notice that some of the options are labeled "Not Bound." In this case, if you want easy access to those commands or functions, you can assign whichever keyboard key or mouse button you want to them.

Select the "X" icon to the right of any key binding to delete it and then reassign that task to an alternate keyboard key or mouse button. To restore all of the key bindings to their default settings, click on the Choose Preset button that's displayed near the bottom-right corner of the screen.

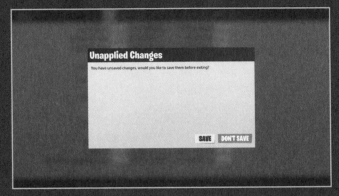

To save your changes after altering anything within this menu, press the ESC key. When the Unapplied Changes pop-up window appears, be sure to select the Save option. If you select the Don't Save option, any changes made will not be saved or applied to the game.

By default, the Windows and Mac versions of *Fortnite: Battle Royale* are designed by be played using a mouse/keyboard combination to control the game. However, you have the option of connecting a compatible PlayStation 4 or Xbox One controller to your computer to control the game using that handheld controller. If you opt to do this, be sure to access the Controller submenu within Settings to choose a controller layout and tweak your controller settings.

As you'll discover later in this section, if you're a PlayStation 4, Xbox One, or Nintendo Switch gamer, you have the option of connecting an optional keyboard and mouse to your console-based gaming system. When you do this, it overrides the controller as being the primary way you'll interact with the game.

Adjusting the Controller Submenu Options

The PlayStation 4, Xbox One, and Nintendo Switch are all designed to allow gamers to control *Fortnite: Battle Royale* using a hand-held controller. It's also possible, however, to connect a PS4 or Xbox One controller to a Windows PC or Mac, or to an iPhone, iPad, or Android-based mobile devices in order to control the game using a controller (as opposed to a keyboard/mouse combo or a mobile device's built-in touchscreen).

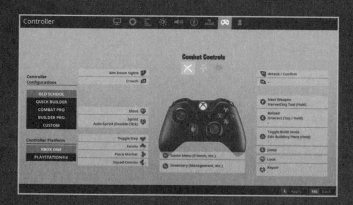

From the Controller submenu within Settings (shown here on a PC), the first option you have is to choose between four main controller layouts—Old School, Quick Builder, Combat Pro, or Builder Pro. Which one you choose is a matter of personal preference. Study each controller layout and choose one that best fits your gaming style.

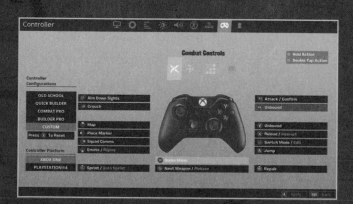

Choose the Custom option to fully customize the layout of the controller. Notice that near the top-center of the screen there are four icons which represent Combat Controls, Build Controls, Edit Controls, and Dead Zone.

The PlayStation 4 version of *Fortnite: Battle Royale* is designed to be played using a standard PS4 wireless controller. The Xbox One version of the game is designed to be played using a standard Xbox One wireless controller.

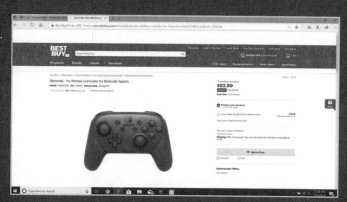

The Nintendo Switch version of the game can be played with the system's Joy-Con controllers, but your gaming experience and control over the game will be vastly improved if you upgrade to the optional Nintendo Switch Pro Controller ($69.99 US).

Later in this chapter, you'll learn about optional replacement controllers from third-party companies, like SCUF Gaming (www.scufgaming.com), that potentially offer more precise control when playing *Fortnite: Battle Royale*.

While most "pro" gamers opt to play *Fortnite: Battle Royale* on a Windows PC using a keyboard/mouse combo, those that use a console-based system often upgrade their controller. Some pro gamers believe that the speed difference between a wireless and corded controller impacts their response time and accuracy during matches. However, this too is a matter of personal preference.

If you opt to use a controller when playing *Fortnite: Battle Royale* on a Windows PC, Mac, iPhone, iPad, or some Android-based mobile devices, you have the option to connecting either a PS4 or Xbox One controller (corded or wireless) to your gaming system. From the Controller submenu within Settings, be sure to select the controller type you're using, in addition to the controller layout.

Take Control of the Game's Audio

Sound effects have always played an essential role in *Fortnite: Battle Royale*. Often, you'll hear weapons fire or enemies approaching, before you can see the danger. Because the sound effects are directional, by listening carefully, you'll be able to determine where sounds (potential dangers) are coming from, as well as the distance they are from your soldier's current location.

Important sound effects to listen for include enemy soldier footsteps, the sound of nearby weapon fire, doors opening/ closing when inside a structure, the roar of a nearby vehicle engine (being driven by an enemy), and the sound of adversaries building. The storm also makes a unique sound, as do chests (shown here) when you're close to them (even if they can't immediately be seen).

Be sure to connect good quality stereo headphones to your gaming system to experience the sound effects the way they were meant to be heard. Headphones will provide more authentic audio, which will give you an advantage during matches. Pay close attention to the volume and direction sound effects are coming from.

Anytime you're playing a Duos or Squads match, or any game play mode that requires you to speak with other gamers, be sure to utilize a gaming headset (with a built-in microphone) in conjunction with your gaming system. This will allow you to clearly hear the game's sound effects, along with the voices of the people you need to communicate with during matches.

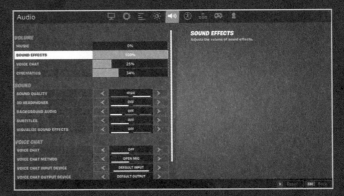

From the Audio submenu within Settings, you're able to customize the volume related to the game's music, sound effects, and voice chat functionality. Many gamers opt to turn off the in-game music altogether, and then boost the Sound Effects and Voice Chat levels.

If you have 3D headphones (virtual surround sound), be sure to turn on the 3D Headphones feature within the Audio submenu to take full advantage of this functionality during gameplay.

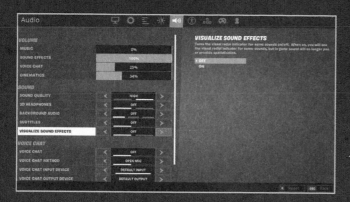

To help you determine the direction sound effects are coming from during matches, if you're having trouble clearly hearing this using your TV or computer's built-in speakers, for example, consider turning on the Visualize Sound Effects feature. This causes a visual radial indicator to be displayed on-screen when sound effects are heard to help you determine the direction those sound effects are originating from.

The Cinematics Volume option refers to the audio level you hear when non-gameplay-related animations are presented in between matches or at the start or end of major in-game Events. These Cinematics don't impact actual game play during matches. Likewise, the Subtitles option applies more to *Fortnite: Save the World*, where in-game, computer-controlled characters speak dialogue that as a gamer you'd need to hear. This doesn't apply in *Fortnite: Battle Royale*.

More Options for Upgrading Your Gaming Gear

This section showcases a wide range of optional products, including gaming keyboards, gaming mice, gaming headsets, and pro-quality controllers that can be used to upgrade your gaming gear in an effort to give you faster response time, more accurate movement and aiming, and greater control when playing *Fortnite: Battle Royale*.

Before spending a fortune upgrading your gaming gear, first make sure you've done everything possible to boost your Internet speed, and then focus on tweaking the options offered by the game's Settings-related menus (particularly those offered within the Video, Game, Controller Sensitivity, Input, and Controller submenus).

Only after you're convinced you've done everything possible within the game itself to enhance your game play experience should you consider upgrading your mouse and keyboard or controller. You already know that using good-quality headphones or a gaming headset will allow you to better and more clearly hear the game's sound effects during matches.

Optional Gaming Keyboards

Several well-known companies, like Corsair, HyperX Gaming, Logitech, Razer, Roccat, and SteelSeries (Apex), offer optional gaming keyboards, gaming mice, and/or keyboard/mouse combos designed for pro gamers.

A few features set gaming keyboards apart from traditional computer keyboards, which is why pro gamers prefer using them. For starts, the best pro-level gaming keyboards are mechanical keyboards. This means that each keyboard key is controlled with its own mechanical switch. This improves durability and response time, reduces "wobble" during quick presses, and provides a tactile feel under the gamer's fingers as individual keys are pressed.

Since you'll be pressing commonly used keys thousands of times per match, often in quick succession, it's essential that the keyboard you use is able to withstand this level of usage, without individual keys sticking or breaking over time.

For a detailed explanation of the high-tech switches built into all Roccat gaming keyboards, check out: https://en.roccat.org/Labs/Titan-Switch.

Most gaming keyboards are wired (as opposed to wireless) to ensure fast and accurate communication between the keyboard and computer (or gaming console). What most gamers love about gaming keyboards, however, is the often customizable, multi-colored LED backlighting within each key.

These colored LEDs can be used for decoration, or customized and assigned to specific keys, so movement-related keys are displayed in one color, while gun controls, throwable weapon controls, item controls, and/or vehicle controls, for example, can each be displayed using a different color for easy visual reference when playing your favorite games, including *Fortnite: Battle Royale*.

When it comes to choosing a gaming keyboard, most offer full-size keys and a traditional 122-key layout. However, some offer a built-in palm rest or a more streamlined design, along with tactile key switches designed for durability and speed. Based on your needs and personal preference, most gaming keyboards come in a wired or wireless configuration.

One feature pro gamers often look for in a gaming keyboard is low-profile keys. This means each key does not need to be pressed as far down in order to register the keystroke, thus potentially saving a small fraction of a second per keystroke. How far a key needs to move to register a keystroke is referred to as "travel distance." For gamers, the lowest possible travel distance for a tactile key is important.

Another speed-related feature to consider when choosing a gaming keyboard is its polling rate. This determines how many times per second the keyboard communicates with the computer or gaming console. The higher the polling rate, the better.

To learn more about pro-level gaming keyboards, visit the websites for these companies:

- **Corsair**—www.corsair.com
- **HyperX Gaming**—www.hyperxgaming.com/us/keyboards
- **Logitech**—www.logitech.com/en-us/keyboards
- **Razer**—www.razer.com/gaming-keyboards
- **Roccat**—https://en.roccat.org/Keyboards
- **SteelSeries (Apex)**—https://steelseries.com/gaming-keyboards

ProSettings.net (https://prosettings.net/best-fortnite-settings-list) offers a detailed listing of the optional equipment used by pro Fortnite gamers that includes the technical specifications for each piece of equipment, as well as the customized in-game settings each gamer uses to get the best response from that equipment.

To further help you adjust the settings related to optional pro-level gaming equipment, ProSettings.net offers a separate webpage for Fortnite gamers that can be found here: https://prosettings.net/best-fortnite-settings-options-guide.

Check out the HyperX Alloy Elite RGB gaming keyboard ($139.99, www.hyperxgaming.com/us/keyboards/alloy-elite-mechanical-gaming-keyboard).

Shown here is the popular Razer Huntsman Tournament Edition gaming keyboard ($129.99, https://www.razer.com/gaming-keyboards-keypads/razer-huntsman-tournament-edition).

The K70 LUX Mechanical Gaming Keyboard from Corsair ($119.99, www.corsair.com/us/en/Categories/Products/Gaming-Keyboards/Mechanical-Gaming-Keyboards/k70-lux-config-na/p/CH-9101020-NA) is one of many that offer colorful LED backlights.

Designed specifically for gamers, the Razer Tartarus Pro ($129.99, www.razer.com/gaming-keyboards-keypads/razer-tartarus-pro) is a one-handed keyboard with 32 programmable keys, LED lighting, and a bunch of other features designed to make controlling the action in games like Fortnite: Battle Royale *easier and more efficient. With a built-in, 8-way directional thumbpad, it's a cross between a controller and keyboard.*

For Xbox One gamers, Razer offers the Turret for Xbox One gaming keyboard and mouse ($249, www.razer.com/gaming-keyboards-keypads/razer-turret-for-xbox-one). However, other optional gaming keyboards and mice can also be linked with most gaming systems using a USB cable or a wireless Bluetooth connection.

Since using a keyboard/mouse combo typically gives a gamer better movement and aiming accuracy control, for example, Epic Games has added programming into *Fortnite: Battle Royale* that matches up console-based gamers using a keyboard/mouse combo with each other, as opposed to matching them up with gamers just using a controller.

Optional Gaming Mice

The same companies that design and manufacture gaming keyboards also offer gaming mice. These are designed to replace the mouse that came bundled with your computer. In addition to having colorful LED lights, gaming mice typically offer a fast polling rate (meaning it communicates more often per second with the computer or gaming console). A good polling rate for a gaming mouse is 1000Hz, meaning it communicates 1,000 times per second with the computer or mobile device it's connected to.

Gaming mice tend to be more ergonomic and some offer extra buttons that can be custom programmed for individual games. Just like with gaming keyboards, gaming mice come in wired or wireless configurations. Once again, some pro gamers believe that the reaction time of wired mice is better and more accurate when playing high-action or combat-intense games, like *Fortnite: Battle Royale*, but a wireless mouse is still a popular and widely used option (even among pro players).

A gaming mouse is designed to be more accurate when it comes to precision movements, offer a smooth and controlled glide over the mouse pad, plus have faster and more durable buttons than traditional mice.

While it is not necessary for a gaming keyboard and gaming mouse to come from the same manufacturer, many gamers prefer to have a matching set. Again, this is a matter of personal preference. Focus on choosing a gaming keyboard and mouse that offers the functionality, durability, quality, and appearance you want and need.

For more information about how speed, accuracy, and durability is measured when it comes to gaming mice, check out this page of Razer's website—www.razer.com/razer-focus-plus-sensor.

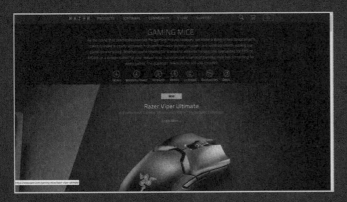

Shown here is the Razer Viper Ultimate gaming mouse ($149.99, www.razer.com/gaming-mice/razer-viper-ultimate). It's one of more than a dozen different mice in the company's gaming mouse lineup. This one offers wireless technology that the company boasts is 25 percent faster than more traditional wireless mice. This mouse also offers low click latency and an extremely precise optical sensor for movement accuracy.

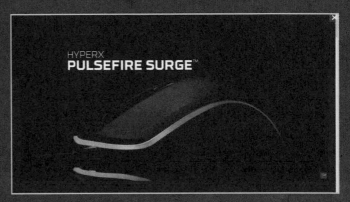

Shown here is the HyperX Pulsefire Surge RGB Gaming Mouse ($54.99, www.hyperxgaming.com/us/mice/pulsefire-surge-rgb-gaming-mouse).

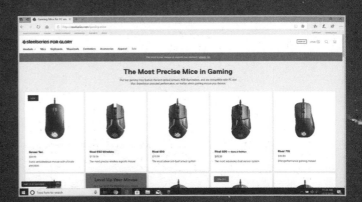

SteelSeries offers more than a dozen different gaming mouse models, ranging in price from $49.99 to $119.99. To help you choose the best one to meet your needs, visit: https://steelseries.com/upgrade-your-mouse.

Pro-Level Controllers

If you're looking for a highly rated, pro-level controller for your PS4 or Xbox One, for example, that could also be used with a PC or mobile device, the following are a few companies that offer viable options.

Keep in mind, you'll likely pay a premium for a pro-level controller, compared to the price of a replacement DualShock 4 ($59.99) from Sony or Xbox One Wireless Controller from Microsoft ($59.99).

Pro-level controller manufacturers include:

- **Astro Gaming**—www.astrogaming.com/en-us/products/controllers.html
- **Nacon Gaming**—www.nacongaming.com
- **Razer**—www.razer.com
- **SCUF**—www.scufgaming.com
- **SteelSeries**—https://steelseries.com/gaming-controllers

According to SCUF Gaming (https://scuf-gaming.com), more than 90 percent of all pro gamers rely on SCUF controllers when completing on a PS4 or Xbox One, for example. This company offers an ever-expanding lineup of optional corded and wireless PS4 and Xbox One controllers, some of which are priced upwards of $199.95 each.

The SCUF Vantage 2 ($184.95, https://scufgaming.com/playstation-vantage-2-controller) for the PS4 and PC, for example, is a highly customizable controller with four rear paddles, a fully adjustable trigger system, and two side-action buttons. Using the free software available for this controller, it's possible to remap up to 15 functions for a truly personalized gaming experience.

The SCUF Prestige ($159.95, https://scufgaming.com/xbox-scuf-prestige-controller) is just one example of the company's several pro-level Xbox One controllers that also includes 14 mappable controller functions, as well as interactable faceplates so you can alter the appearance of your controller with ease. The controller's battery lasts about 30 hours per charge and can be used as a wired or wireless controller.

Keep in mind, a wireless controller uses a rechargeable battery that needs to be recharged after a pre-determined number of hours. So if you only have one controller, be sure to keep it fully charged so you can enjoy marathon gaming sessions without worrying that your controller battery will go dead during a match. For example, the Sony DualShock 4 controller's battery life is between four and eight hours per charge. You can often extend a controller's battery life by turning off the vibration feature.

The Razer Wolverine Tournament Edition for Xbox One ($119.99, www.razer.com/gaming-controllers/razer-wolverine-tournament-edition) is a pro-level gaming controller designed specifically for eSports professionals.

Based on the size of your hands and your personal gaming style, if you plan to upgrade your controller, choose one that offers the ergonomics, customizability, battery life, and the ability to shorten your response times. Consider the weight and shape of the controller; the quality of the buttons, triggers, and thumbsticks; the battery life; and whether or not you want and need a wired or wireless controller.

There are many generic and low-cost replacement controllers available for the PS4, Xbox One, and Nintendo Switch—which can also be used with a computer or mobile device—but if the controller was not designed from the ground up for serious gaming, your experience playing *Fortnite: Battle Royale* could be hindered by some lower cost, poor quality controller alternatives.

Link a Wireless Controller with Your iPhone or iPad

Compared to the touchscreen built into the Apple iPhone and iPad, many gamers feel that using a controller when playing *Fortnite* offers must better control over the game. If you want to link a wireless PS4 or Xbox One controller with your iOS mobile device to control *Fortnite: Battle Royale*, this is now possible thanks to the iOS 13 operating system that's built into your mobile device.

To establish the link between the controller and mobile device, activate your controller and place it in pairing mode. To do this, using a PlayStation 4 (wireless) Dualshock 4 controller, press and hold the PS button and Share button on the controller until the light bar begins to flash. On an Xbox One controller, press and hold down the "XBox" button along with the Wireless button (on the front of the controller) to place it in pairing mode.

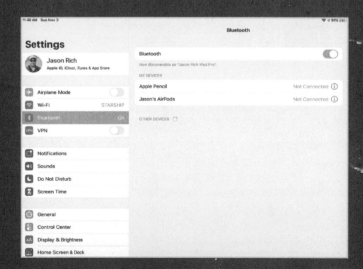

On your iPhone or iPad (shown here), launch Settings and select the Bluetooth option. Turn on the virtual switch associated with the Bluetooth option.

Once the Bluetooth menu within Settings (on your iPhone or iPad) says that the controller (in this case the DualShock 4 Wireless Controller) is connected, exit out of Settings and launch Fortnite.

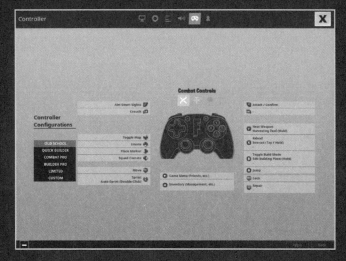

From the Settings menu within Fortnite, tap on the Controller tab displayed near the top-center of the screen. From the Controller menu screen (shown here on an iPad Pro), select your controller layout. Exit out of Settings to return to the Lobby. From there, choose a game play mode and kick off a match.

For Android-based smartphones, Razer offers its Junglecat Dual-Sided Gaming Controller ($99.99, www.razer.com/gaming-controllers/razer-junglecat) and Raiju Mobile gaming controller ($149.99, www.razer.com/gaming-controllers/razer-raiju-mobile).

Gaming Headsets

When it comes to experiencing a *Fortnite: Battle Royale* Solo match, any good quality stereo headphones will provide significantly better sound compared to using the speakers built into your television set or monitor.

Headphones or ear buds, for example, range in price from under $30.00 to several hundred dollars, with the more expensive options offering features like 3D sound (virtual surround sound) and noise cancelling. Anytime you need to speak with your fellow gamers during a Duos, Squads, or Team-oriented match, you'll definitely want to experience *Fortnite: Battle Royale* using an optional gaming headset with a built-in microphone.

In addition to the audio and microphone quality offered by an optional gaming headset, you'll need to choose between a corded or wireless model. Since you'll likely be wearing the headset for hours at a time during marathon gaming sessions, the weight of the headset and its comfort should definitely be considered.

For a good quality gaming headset, plan on spending between $100.00 and $300.00 (US). Shown here, the Turtle Beach Elite Atlas Aero for Windows (www.turtlebeach.com/pages/elite-atlas-aero-headset), for example, is priced at $149.95. It provides an immersive, 3D audio experience that'll help you feel like you're actually on the island with the combat action happening all around you when playing Fortnite: Battle Royale.

Priced at $129.99, the HyperX Cloud Alpha S Gaming Headset (www.hyperxgaming.com/us/headsets/cloud-alpha-s-gaming-headset) offers award-winning technology that provides for a virtual 7.1 surround sound listening experience. You're able to manually adjust the bass levels, while balancing the game and voice chat volumes, for example.

Some of the best-known gaming headset companies include:

- **Corsair**—www.corsair.com/us/en/Categories/Products/Gaming-Headsets/c/Cor_Products_HeadSets
- **HyperX Gaming**—www.hyperxgaming.com/us/headsets
- **Logitech**—www.logitech.com/en-us/headsets
- **Razer**—www.razer.com/gaming-headsets-and-audio
- **SteelSeries**—https://steelseries.com/gaming-headsets
- **Turtle Beach**—www.turtlebeach.com

When experiencing Fortnite: Battle Royale on most Bluetooth-compatible gaming systems or mobile devices, another option is to utilize the same wireless earbuds you already use with your smartphone. These too have a built-in microphone, so they can be used when playing any of Fortnite: Battle Royale's game play modes.

Apple's 2nd generation AirPods ($159.00 or $199.00 US, www.apple.com/airpods-2nd-generation), or the newer AirPods Pro ($249.00 US, www.apple.com/airpods-pro) ear buds are popular options. The AirPods Pro, for example, offer advanced noise cancelling technology built into the wireless earbuds, which allow you to eliminate outside ambient noise if you're playing Fortnite: Battle Royale in a noisy room, for example.

A slightly lower cost option are Amazon's EchoBuds ($129.00 US, www.amazon.com/dp/B07F6VM1S3), which also offer an active noise reduction feature.

The thing to consider when using wireless ear buds as an audio option when playing games is battery life. Especially when you're using the built-in microphone and listening to the game's audio, the battery life of the EchoBuds, for example, averages about five hours per charge, while the AirPods Pro offers about 4.5 hours of listening time per charge.

Keep in mind, traditional wireless gaming headsets offer a longer battery life per charge, while corded headsets use power from the console or computer and have no rechargeable battery to deal with.

SECTION 3

FINE-TUNE YOUR *FORTNITE: BATTLE ROYALE* GAMING SKILLS

While Loot Lake was once the main body of water on the mysterious island, the new island layout includes multiple lakes, many of which are interconnected by rivers. To help your soldier quickly navigate around these waterways, speed boats that are capable of shooting projectile weapons were made available.

The transition between *Fortnite: Battle Royale* Season 10 and Chapter 2, Season 1 was dramatic. In fact, Epic Games introduced what many consider to be a radically different battle royale-style game.

The core objectives when playing a *Fortnite: Battle Royale* Solo, Duos, or Squads match remain pretty much the same as before, but Chapter 2 features an almost entirely new island map, new weapons, several new healing items, new vehicles, new tools, and a wide range of new strategies you'll need to master if you want to achieve #1 Victory Royale.

If you've acquired a seasonal Battle Pass, how you'll unlock the reward associated with each of the 100 Tiers has also once again been revamped and is now based more on earning XP (Experience Points) and completing specific mission and challenges.

Soldiers can walk through shallow water and swim (rather quickly) in deeper water while still holding a weapon. Anytime your soldier is traveling through water, however, they're rather unprotected from enemy attacks, so you'll need to be ready to fire your weapon(s) or take evasive maneuvers quickly.

By submerging your soldier in water and keeping still, you can remain somewhat hidden. When an enemy comes close, you can leap from the water with your soldier's gun blazing to launch a surprise attack.

Within lakes and rivers, you're apt to discover all sorts of loot items and weapons, but to acquire them, you'll need to go fishing. Fishing rods are a commonly available item. Simply by casting the fishing line into a body of water where you see fish swimming around, you'll be able to catch fish (which are typically used to boost your soldier's Health and Shield meters), plus discover other useful loot items and weapons.

The land-based terrain is also rather different from what experienced *Fortnite: Battle Royale* gamers were previously accustomed to. As a result, even the most skilled gamers will

need to get fully reacquainted with the island and explore all of the new points of interest.

As always, choosing the best landing location remains a vital strategy, based on your personal gaming style and objectives. Upon landing, finding and gathering a well-rounded arsenal, along with an ample supply of ammo for your weapons, continues to be essential. While exploring the island and potentially engaging enemies in combat, keeping your soldier's Health and Shield meters as full as possible will help to ensure your soldier's extended survival during matches.

Familiar Health and Shield replenishment items, like Shield Potions, Med Kits, and Bandages continue to be available, but Chapter 2 introduced additional ways to give your soldier's Health and Shield meters a boost. For example, in addition to catching fish, wading in Slurpy Swamp's contaminated water (shown here) will also activate or replenish your soldier's Shield meter.

This section focuses on tips and strategies that'll help you fine-tune, update, and improve your overall gaming skills when it comes to playing *Fortnite: Battle Royale*.

Whatever You Do, Do It Quickly!

Whether you're launching an attack, taking cover from an incoming attack, building, avoiding the storm, or doing pretty much anything else during a match, there's rarely any time to just kick back and dawdle. Especially when soldiers are evenly matched, it's typically the gamer with a speed advantage who comes out ahead.

Learn to think fast and react even faster. You'll need to practice quickly switching between weapons, reloading your weapons (assuming you have an ample supply of ammo), and being able to accurately aim and fire weapons at your target(s).

Speed is also essential when building, editing, and repairing structures, especially when you need a protective barrier against incoming attacks or you need to achieve a height advantage over a nearby enemy.

Simply traveling from one location to another also requires you to constantly keep moving, especially when you're out in the open and vulnerable to attacks from all directions (including above or below your soldier's location).

There will be times when you think you're alone in an area, but as soon as you let your guard down, you'll discover an enemy is spying on you from a distance and has a long-range (scoped) weapon or a projectile weapon targeting you. Thus, it's always important to approach chests, Loot Llamas, and Supply Drops with extreme caution.

Meanwhile, if you're taking a few minutes to do some fishing, for example, be ready to quickly switch from holding and using a fishing rod to grabbing and aiming a weapon from your soldier's inventory.

Instead of standing out in the open when fishing (and being vulnerable to an attack from all sides), consider building a structure with an opening that faces that water, but that protects you from all other sides (including above you).

Gathering and harvesting resources (wood, stone, and metal) continues to be an important task during matches. You'll need these resources to build with, as well as to upgrade your weapons, for example. Harvesting resources requires using your soldier's Harvesting Tool.

Your soldier's Harvesting Tool can also be used as a close-range weapon in a pinch, but it won't inflict too much damage with each swipe. Thus, you'll need to practice quickly switching from your Harvesting Tool to a weapon and switching from Combat mode (where you're using a weapon) to Building mode (which allows you to build structures).

In addition to lots of practice, the best way to improve your speed and reaction time during a match is to memorize the keyboard keys and mouse buttons or controller buttons, so you won't have to think about what button to press each time you need to control your soldier or utilize an in-game feature or function. The best *Fortnite: Battle Royale* gamers have fine-tuned and perfected their game-specific muscle memory.

Select an Overall Approach to Each Match

Mastering *Fortnite: Battle Royale* requires you to perfect a wide range of gaming skills and simultaneously juggle multiple responsibilities during each and every match. Since very few gamers are experts at every single aspect of the game, most choose to focus in on what they're really good at, and adapt their overall strategy based on those strengths.

Right at the start of each match, you can choose one of three overall strategies.

Strategy #1—Choose a Popular Landing Location

One option is to choose a landing spot that'll place your soldier right in the middle of a popular point of interest on the island. This strategy is best suited for more experienced and highly skilled gamers, because it virtually guarantees that you'll encounter enemies right away and be forced to engage in combat, sometimes within seconds after landing.

To achieve success when you adopt this strategy, it's best to land in a location that you already know extremely well. Try landing on top of a building's roof, or somewhere high up, and select a spot where you're confident you'll be able to grab at least one weapon (and some ammo) right away.

Knowing that you've chosen a popular landing spot, select a location to touch down where you'll be able to take cover quickly, especially if you can't immediately grab a weapon. While you're still in the air, study the ground below and try to spot weapons lying out in the open that you will be able to grab right away. Shown here, there's a Pump Shotgun and some ammo on the roof of a building located in the heart of Steamy Stacks.

While your soldier is still in midair, if you notice other soldiers planning to land at your desired landing spot, or you see enemies have already landed where you planned to touch down, quickly veer off and find an alternate landing spot. If you're not the first soldier to land at a specific location, you'll often find yourself at a huge disadvantage, especially if the enemy is able to grab a weapon and target you before you've even landed.

Remember, when your soldier lands, they're unarmed (except for their Harvesting Tool). If an enemy already has a weapon, they can shoot from a distance and take you out within moments after you've landed, often before you even have time to take cover or grab a weapon.

Strategy #2—Land Just Outside a Popular Landing Location

Instead of landing right in the heart of a popular point of interest and likely being forced to confront enemies immediately, consider landing just outside a popular point of interest. You'll often discover areas that overlook popular locations that contain weapons, ammo, and loot items—either lying out in the open, or within chests and ammo boxes, for example.

By landing just outside a popular point of interest, you'll have a few moments to build up your soldier's arsenal, explore your immediate surroundings, and study what's happening within the nearby point of interest before you enter it. Not only will you then be able to enter into that area better armed and prepared for combat, but you'll have allowed your enemies to fight amongst themselves and potentially eliminate some of the dangers before you arrive.

Ideally, choose a landing location that gives you a height advantage, so you're able to look down upon the point of interest you plan to visit. One benefit to this approach is that if you're able to find a weapon with a scope or a long-range projectile weapon, you can target enemies from a distance and clear your path before traveling into the desired point of interest.

Strategy #3—Select a More Remote Landing Location

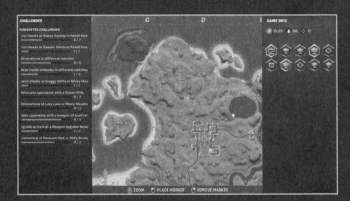

Especially if you're a newb, one of the safest approaches you can take early in a match is to land in a remote location, far away from popular points of interest. This often gives you plenty of time to explore the area, gather a well-rounded and powerful arsenal, harvest resources, and start preparing early on for the End Game portion of a match.

When you land in an area where you're not apt to encounter enemies early on, this means you can initially focus your energies on objectives other than combat and survival. Of course, there's always a chance you'll encounter one or two random enemies, but as long as you have a weapon in hand, or you take evasive action to avoid them, you can enjoy the first few minutes of a match without engaging in combat.

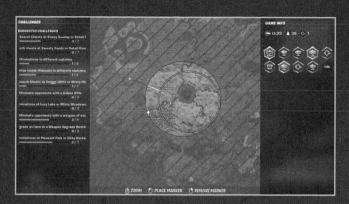

One potential drawback to landing in a remote location is that you won't know where the storm will initially form and move until after you've landed. Thus, it may be necessary to travel a far distance rather early in the match to avoid the storm. Be sure to keep an eye on the mini-map, or check the Island Map several times during the first few minutes of the match, and then determine the best route to take to stay clear of the storm while also avoiding potentially heavily populated areas. Shown here, the soldier is stuck in the storm outside of Sweaty Sands and must make their way toward Salty Springs before their Health meter gets depleted.

In general, if you land close to the center of the island, as opposed to somewhere along the outskirts, your chances of having to travel great distances to avoid the storm decrease. However, you could get lucky when you land in a remote location. You might discover that the safe area of the island will be in or near your current location once the storm forms and begins to expand.

Pay attention to the mini-map and follow the white line that appears to help you reach the safe area of the island and avoid the deadly storm. Once the storm gets too close, it's often hard, if not impossible, to outrun it on foot, so make sure you have an exit strategy in mind that involves the use of a vehicle or another mode of travel.

Assuming you've landed in a remote location, as soon as the storm forms, you can begin following the path to safety, but along the way, pick up weapons, ammo, and loot items, and perhaps harvest some resources, while making a point to avoid enemy confrontations by hiding if you see or hear enemies approaching.

Listen Carefully to What's Happening Around You

No matter where you are on the island, or what you're doing, always listen carefully for the sounds generated by approaching enemies. Listen for footsteps, weapon fire, the sound of an enemy building a structure, doors opening or closing (if you're within a structure), or the sound of approaching vehicles being driven by enemies. Almost all vehicles that can be driven or ridden in *Fortnite: Battle Royale* make a lot of noise when they're in motion.

Not only will you sometimes hear enemies and impending danger from a distance, you'll often hear threats before you can see them, so always listen carefully to what's happening around you.

At the same time, pay attention to the sounds your soldier generates. Keep in mind, especially within a building or structure, tiptoeing (crouching) generates less noise than walking. Running generates the most noise. Using your Harvesting Tool to smash objects, especially metal objects and vehicles, generates a lot of noise, as does opening and closing doors.

Driving a vehicle around the island will allow you to get from one place to another quickly, but it'll also attract a lot of attention from nearby enemies, who can launch attacks on the vehicle you're traveling in. Most types of long-range projectile weapons can be used to take out or destroy a moving vehicle from far away, while a sniper rifle (or weapon with a scope) can be used to target the driver or a passenger within a vehicle, also from a distance.

Get to Know the New Terrain

The island map encompasses a lot of terrain and many new points of interest. The island also continues to evolve, as new locations are often added as part of a weekly game update or patches. In addition, with each new gaming season, you can expect significant changes to the island.

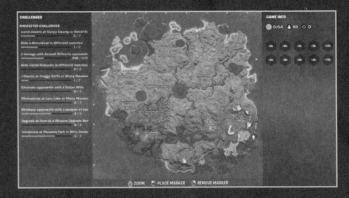

At the start of Season 2, Chapter 1, the island map contained 13 labeled points of interest, as well as many areas in between those points of interest that contained random buildings, structures, bridges, roads, and rivers, for example. If you're a veteran Fortnite: Battle Royale gamer, you may have recognized Salty Springs, Retail Row, and Pleasant Park as three familiar points of interest (although each experienced some modification). The remaining areas of the island were mostly brand new.

Some new points of interest contain new items you can take advantage of. For example, within Slurpy Swamp, you'll discover metal canisters. When you destroy one of these objects using your soldier's Harvesting Tool, you'll boost your soldier's Shield meter.

When exploring the Slurpy Swamp area, if your soldier simply stands still in the contaminated (discolored) water, their Shield meter will slowly get replenished. Thus, choosing this point of interest as your landing spot at the start of a match virtually guarantees you'll be able to boost your soldier's Shield meter to 100 percent very quickly. As always, however, Shields will protect your soldier from incoming weapon attacks and explosions, but not from falls or damage from the storm.

Ideally, you want to memorize every inch of the island, so you know how to safely navigate around, quickly find places to hide, and position your soldier in the best spots to launch attacks. Becoming familiar with the various points of interest will also help you quickly determine when and where you're most likely to discover weapons, ammo, loot items, vehicles, and chests, for example.

Realistically, memorizing every inch of the island is going to take a lot of time. Instead, you're better off focusing on getting well acquainted with just a handful of locations in various parts of the island, so you'll be comfortable spending time in your favorite locations and have a better chance of defeating enemies while you're there.

Of course, the random direction the Battle Bus follows as it travels over the island at the start of a match, and then the formation and movement of the storm, will force you to move into areas you may not be as familiar with, so you'll need to adapt.

Since you know specific locations on the island change often, instead of focusing on memorizing each and every point of interest, as well as the areas of the island in between the points of interest, focus on learning how to survive in various types of terrain.

As you'll discover, the same strategies can be used for survival, exploration, and fighting anytime you're in a city or urban area that's filled with buildings located close together. Here you know you'll need to use close-range fighting techniques and likely have to explore within various types of multi-level buildings and structures.

Each type of terrain has its own benefits and disadvantages. For example, traveling over hills and mountains potentially gives you a natural height advantage over enemies below.

Farmland typically means you'll need to travel across vast and wide open terrain, which can be dangerous and leave your soldier vulnerable.

Haystacks located in the farm areas can be climbed on or hidden within in a way that'll keep your soldier out of your enemy's sights. Of course, knowing that soldiers can be hidden within haystacks, it makes sense to shoot into them or toss explosives at them if you're searching the area looking for enemies.

It's also possible for soldiers to hide within some metal dumpsters. When your soldier faces the dumpster, press the Hide button to jump inside and hide.

Anytime you need to cross wide open spaces, move fast, travel in a zigzag pattern, and keep having your soldier jump up and down to make them a difficult moving target to hit. Also be prepared to quickly build walls or a mini structure around your soldier for added protection against incoming attacks.

Areas that contain factories or very large structures will require you to spend a lot of time indoors exploring, while suburban areas will contain individual homes and smaller structures that you'll often want to explore within, but you will typically need to travel outside (at ground level) to get from one structure or building to the next.

Anytime you're at the top of a hill or mountain and need to get back down to ground level quickly, never just leap off of a ledge or cliff, unless you have an item to active that ensures a safe landing. In general, you want to slide down the edge of a hill or mountain to avoid a potentially fatal injury.

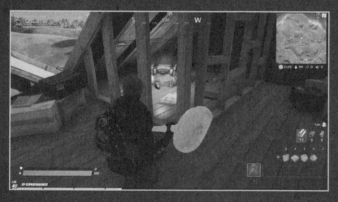

In general, your soldier can survive a fall from up to two or three stories with little or no injury. Falls from higher can be catastrophic. Don't forget, you always have the ability to build a ramp or stairs to help you climb up or down a hill, or quickly reach the top or bottom of a structure without jumping. You're also able to build bridges to help you cross horizontally from one location to another, such as between tall buildings or across large bodies of water.

In general, when exploring homes and some other types of buildings, you're most apt to find the best weapons and loot items (as well as chests, for example) within an attic or basement.

Meanwhile, with so much of the island now covered in water, you'll likely need to walk across streams and rivers, swim within lakes, or drive a speedboat. Traveling in open water leaves you vulnerable to attack from soldiers positioned on land who will often use long-range weapons to attack from a distance.

Whenever possible, use the terrain where you are to your advantage. Look for objects you can hide or crouch behind for protection. Starting in Chapter 2, Season 1, the island offered a variety of objects, such as dumpsters and haystacks, that a soldier can hide within to remain entirely out of sight. Bushes also remain a viable hiding spot.

Based on your strategy and what you'll need out of the landing spot, choose the most appropriate place to land. Pleasant Park continues to offer a wide range of benefits. For example, you'll find buildings and objects made of all sorts of materials which are good for harvesting into resources. The homes and small buildings, as well as the parks in the area, often contain chests. Of course, you'll want to focus your search for chests in the basements and attics of the homes.

Large power plants, like Steamy Stacks, are typically chock full of resources to harvest. You'll often find chests, along with plenty of weapons and loot items lying out in the open on the ground. Keep your eyes peeled for a Weapon Upgrade Station in the area.

In heavily wooded areas, like Weeping Woods, you can hide behind trees and use them for cover or harvest them to collect wood.

If you need to leave Steamy Stacks quickly, jump into the pink liquid that gives off steam, and ride the steam up and out of the power plant's towers.

There are several land regions on the island that are along water. Here you're apt to find fishing rods, so you can do some fishing. Keep in mind, these tend to be flat areas of terrain, so when your soldier is not inside of a building, they'll likely be out in the open and vulnerable to potential attack from all directions.

Get the Most Out of Your Trip Aboard the Battle Bus

After selecting the Play option, your soldier gets transported automatically to the pre-deployment area. You'll hang out here for a few minutes while waiting for up to 99 other gamers to join the match.

While in the pre-deployment area you can explore, interact with other soldiers (using emotes), or collect weapons and practice shooting, for example. Anything you collect while in the pre-deployment area gets left behind once your soldier boards the Battle Bus.

The Battle Bus is a blue flying bus that transports all 100 soldiers from the pre-deployment area to the mysterious island. There's just one catch . . . the Battle Bus does not land. Instead, as the bus is flying over the island, you must choose when your soldier should leap from the bus and freefall toward the island.

As the Battle Bus is flying over the island, use the directional controls to look backward, behind the bus. You'll be able to see rival soldiers leap from the bus. Doing this can help you determine where the majority of the enemy soldiers will be landing.

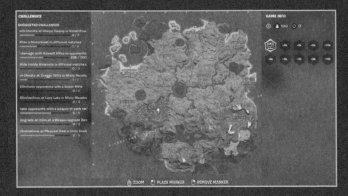

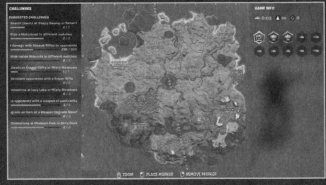

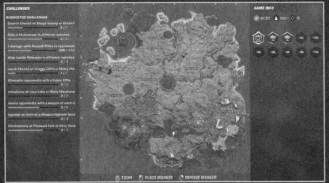

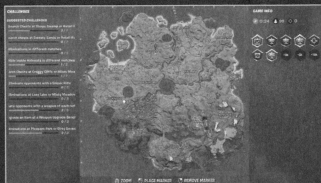

Either while waiting in the pre-deployment area, or during your flight on the Battle Bus, consider checking the Island Map. You'll notice that a blue line, comprised of arrow icons, displays the random route the Battle Bus will be taking over the island, as well as the direction the bus will travel. Use this information to help you choose the perfect time to leap from the bus so you can reach your desired landing location.

Points of interest located near the very start of the route that the Battle Bus will take tend to be very popular, so when you land on the island, you're almost guaranteed to encounter enemy soldiers right away.

Destinations located at the very end of the route that the Battle Bus follows also tend to be popular landing destinations. You can also count on points of interest located near the center of the map always being popular landing spots. Other popular landing spots tend to be the newest points of interest that were most recently added to the map.

Remember, any time you land within a popular point of interest, you'll very likely encounter enemy soldiers right away. For this reason, it's essential that during your soldier's freefall, you guide them as quickly as possible to your desired landing spot. Do this by pointing your soldier straight downward, using the navigational controls.

If you're the first soldier to land at a specific location, you'll likely have a few seconds to quickly find and grab a weapon and ammo, so you can help your soldier protect themselves as rival soldiers land shortly after. However, when your soldier is not the first one to land at a particular spot, the risk of getting shot and eliminated from the match within seconds after landing increases dramatically.

During freefall, moments before your soldier is about to land on the island, their Glider will automatically deploy. This slows down the rate of descent and ensures a safe landing. When the Glider is activated, you'll have better navigational control, allowing you to choose a very precise landing spot.

Remember, while you're still in the air, be on the lookout for weapons lying out in the open that your soldier can land near and quickly grab. If you spot the glow of a chest, that's even better. Chests contain multiple items that can include weapons, ammo, and other loot items, including items used to replenish your soldier's Health and Shield meters.

In addition to looking for weapons just prior to landing on the island, keep your eyes peeled for enemy soldiers who have landed before you. If you spot another soldier, try to veer in another direction and choose an alternate landing spot, since the soldier who already landed (or who will be landing before you) will likely already be armed with a weapon.

Ways to Maintain a Height Advantage Over Adversaries

It's almost always easier to attack an enemy if you're higher up than they are and able to shoot down at them (or toss explosives down toward them). Keeping this in mind, there are numerous ways to maintain a height advantage, regardless of what type of terrain your soldier is in. Here are some popular ways to obtain a height advantage over your enemies.

Build a ramp or a tall structure. If you build a tall ramp that's not reinforced, an enemy can simply shoot and destroy a single tile near the bottom of the ramp and the whole thing will come crashing down, along with your soldier who is standing on it.

Climb to the top of a building, house, or tall structure (or land there) and attack enemies from the roof. Use your soldier's Harvesting Tool to smash through the roof and land inside the structure on the top floor. In a house, this will typically be the attic.

If you need to cross from one building to another, instead of first returning to ground level, build a bridge between roofs of the two structures and then cross it.

Stand at the top of a hill, mountain, or cliff. To gain even more height, build a structure on top of it. Shown here is a three-story 1x1 fortress built on top of a hill. It's constructed using a combination of wood and stone.

When inside a building or structure, get to the top of a stairwell or platform, so you can look and shoot down at enemies on a lower level. By positioning yourself correctly and gaining the element of surprise, you'll often be able to shoot enemies as they're climbing the stairs and eliminate them before they have time to aim their own weapon.

Exploration and Survival Strategies

When necessary, use objects or structures that already exist to hide behind or climb on top of. For example, you can crouch down behind a broken down vehicle, hide behind a tree or rock formation, or use the side of a building for protection against incoming attacks.

Walk, Run, Crouch, and Jump Around the Island

Often when you're exploring the island and visiting various points of interest, you'll need to get from one place to another by traveling on foot. Your soldier has the ability to walk, run, jump, or crouch (tiptoe).

Running allows your soldier to move the fastest, but the sound of footsteps your soldier generates will be the loud. Walking is a bit slower, but quieter. Crouching down (tiptoeing) has two advantage. While it's a very slow way to move around, your soldier will make very little noise, plus their aim will greatly improve when using almost any type of gun to target and shoot enemies while moving.

Take Advantage of Transportation Options

At the start of Chapter 2, Season 1, the majority of transportation options and vehicles that were previously available on the island were vaulted. Of course, they could be re-introduced into the game at any time.

The transportation items that were available at the start of Chapter 2 included speed boats and Zip Lines. While speed boats were pretty easy to find, Ziplines were much less common than ever before.

On the plus side, soldiers can now swim (rather quickly) within water, and while speed boats are the most maneuverable in water, they can also be driven (albeit slowly) across flat land as well. Since high-speed transportation options are less common now than ever before, it's more important than ever to pay attention to the location of the storm and to keep tabs on where and when it's expanding and moving so you can help your soldier avoid it.

It is possible to swim (especially when traveling downstream with the current) faster than your soldier can run on land. This can be useful if you need to put distance between you and an enemy or get away from the approaching storm.

While in the water swimming, your soldier is able to boost their speed if you perfectly time their dives (by pressing the Jump button). With perfect timing, your soldier can swim like a dolphin by leaping out of the water while swimming to pick up speed.

Explore within Buildings and Structures

When you're in an area that contains multiple buildings or structures in close proximity, hide out in one building or structure and then target your scoped weapon through the window and aim at enemies in another building.

Anytime you walk up to a building or structure and you think someone might be inside, don't just approach the door and enter. First peek through a nearby window, if possible, to make sure the coast is clear. Crouch down as you approach a building or structure to make less noise.

When approaching an already open door, move in from an angle. Don't approach the door head on. If someone is waiting inside to shoot, your soldier won't be in the direct line of fire. One option is to toss an explosive weapon through the doorway or have a gun in hand and ready to shoot as you enter.

Since most gamers will make a point to guard the front door of a building or structure, one way to avoid a confrontation is to enter through a backdoor or climb up to the roof from the outside (using a ramp, for example), and then smash your way through the ceiling to get inside. Any approach you take that is not obvious will typically give you a tactical advantage.

If you get pinned within a room of a house or building, crouch down, hide behind an object (or build walls within the room you're in), and then stay still with your weapon pointed at the door. As soon as the enemy opens the door to enter, start firing. Pay attention to which way the door opens so your attack is not blocked by the door.

Just about every structure, house, or building offers areas that make great hiding spots. As long as enemies don't hear you moving around, it's pretty easy to launch a surprise attack from a hiding spot. Keep in mind, if you toss an explosive weapon, it might bounce off a solid object or take a few seconds to detonate, so plan accordingly and don't get caught in your own explosion.

Close Doors Behind You

Anytime you encounter an open door in Fortnite: Battle Royale, this is an indication someone else has already been through that area . . . and they could still be in the vicinity, so proceed with caution.

To confuse your enemies, it's always a good idea to close doors behind you. Then if you sense an enemy is nearby, stand still, hide behind an object, crouch down, and wait for the enemy to approach so you can launch a surprise attack. Any movement on your part could give away your location, because the enemy will likely hear your footsteps.

Shoot Enemies as They Exit Buildings

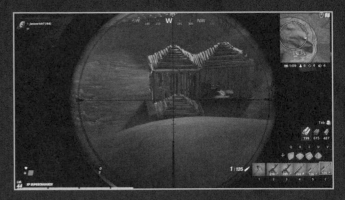

From a sniper's perch located a distance from a building or structure where enemy soldiers are hiding or looting, you're often able to shoot enemies who are inside a building by aiming through a window. Another option is to use a weapon's scope to target the door of a building or structure and wait for the enemy to leave. By waiting for the enemy's exit, you give them time to first collect whatever weapons, ammo, and loot items are within that building. Then, when you defeat that enemy, everything they were carrying drops to the ground and is now yours to collect.

Gather Your Weapon Arsenal & Inventory

At any given time, your soldier has five inventory slots available in their main inventory which can be used to hold various types of guns, explosives, or Health/Shield replenishment items, for example. A sixth inventory slot is always set aside for your soldier's Harvesting Tool. This item cannot be moved or dropped. On most gaming systems, your soldier's inventory slots are displayed near the bottom-right corner of the screen. Once your soldier's inventory slots get filled up, if you come across additional weapons or items you want to take possession of, you'll need to first give something up.

Keep in mind, certain items and weapons, such as Traps, do not require an inventory slot. These items get stored within your soldier's backpack, along with the ammo and resources you collect.

At any time during a match, you're able to switch from the main game screen to your soldier's Backpack Inventory screen. From here, you can rearrange what's in each of your soldier's inventory slots, drop (or share) items you no longer need, and see information about the weapons, items, tools, and ammo currently in your possession.

Each of the *Fortnite: Battle Royale* weapons fall into one of the following categories:

Close-Range Weapons—Pistols are an example of a close-range weapon. These are best used when you're fighting within a structure, and you're not too far away from your target. As you get farther away from your target, the weapon will become harder to aim and inflict less damage. Pistols tend to be the weakest guns in the game. When you have the opportunity to switch them out for a more powerful close- to mid-range weapon, do so.

Several weapons/items, like the Bandage Bazooka, requires two inventory slots to carry the weapon around. Only utilize this valuable space if you have a definite need for this weapon (assuming it is still available within the game and has not been vaulted). In addition to allowing your soldier to share Bandages with allies during a Duos, Squads, or Team-oriented match, for example, you can shoot Bandages from this weapon, and then have your own soldier pick them up and use them on themselves.

Mid-Range Weapons—These tend to be more versatile than close-range weapons, so they can be used with decent accuracy in a broader range of indoor or outdoor combat scenarios.

Long-Range Weapons—Sniper Rifles with a scope are just one example of a long-range weapon that shoots bullets with extreme accuracy when you're far away from your target. When using any weapon with a scope, if you just point the gun and shoot, you'll experience less accuracy than if you press the Aim button, position your enemy within the targeting crosshairs, and then fire the gun.

Explosive Weapons—As you explore the island, you'll be able to find, grab, store, and then use a variety of throwable explosive weapons, such as Grenades. These tend to work best when you're mid-range from your opponent, since you don't want your soldier to be too close to the explosion that occurs once one of these weapons detonate.

Explosive Projectile Weapons Launchers—Anytime you need to destroy buildings, structures, or vehicles, for example, as well as the enemies within them, projectile explosive weapons allow you to target enemies from a distance, and then shoot explosive ammo with extreme accuracy.

A Rocket Launcher is an example of a powerful explosive projectile weapon that uses Rockets as its ammo.

Traps and Specialty Weapons—During each gaming season, a different selection of Traps and specialty weapons are made available. A Trap, for example, can be placed on any flat surface, such as a floor, ceiling, or wall of a structure. Depending on the type of Trap being used, an enemy that gets caught in one could be instantly defeated or at least injured.

Get to Know What Weapons Are Available

During all seasons of *Fortnite: Battle Royale* Chapter 1, each available weapon was only available in certain rankings—Common (grey), Uncommon (green), Rare (blue), Epic (purple), or Legendary (orange/gold). The ranking helped determine a weapon's overall strength and capabilities.

Starting in Chapter 2, Season 1, all available weapons are potentially available in (or can be upgrade to) any ranking, with a few minor exceptions. As a result, fewer different types of weapons are available at any given time.

When building up your arsenal, try to collect weapons with the highest ranking possible, and then locate a Weapon Upgrade Bench and use resources to upgrade the weapons currently in your soldier's inventory.

How to Upgrade Your Weapons

Weapon Upgrade Benches, like this one, are scattered throughout the island. At least during Chapter 2, Season 1, there are more than 20 of them. To take advantage of a Weapon Upgrade Bench, approach it with the weapon you want to upgrade already selected and in your soldier's hands.

A Weapon Upgrade Bench is only useful if you have the right amount of wood, stone, and metal in your soldier's inventory to upgrade one or more of the weapons your soldier is currently carrying. As you can see here, this Uncommon (green) weapon is about to be upgraded to a Rare (blue) weapon at a cost of 150 wood, 150 stone, and 150 metal. Press the Upgrade Weapon button to make this happen.

How many of each resource (wood, stone, and metal) you'll need to upgrade a weapon will depend on its current ranking.

- Upgrading a single Common weapon to an Uncommon weapon requires 50 wood, 50 stone, and 50 metal.
- Upgrading a single Uncommon weapon to a Rare weapon requires 150 wood, 150 stone, and 150 metal.
- Upgrading a single Rare weapon to an Epic weapon requires 250 wood, 250 stone, and 250 metal.
- Upgrading a single Epic weapon to a Legendary weapon requires 350 wood, 350 stone, and 350 metal.

Learn to Accurately Aim Your Weapon(s)

Whenever you point a gun at a target, you'll see aiming crosshairs (also known as a Targeting Box) appear over that target. The size of this box will vary, based on your soldier's movement while aiming the weapon. In general, when you shoot a weapon, the bullets will land somewhere within that hit box or within the crosshairs. If you look carefully, you can see the targeting crosshairs for this weapon against the wall in front of the soldier.

To ensure a direct hit that'll cause maximum damage, you want the targeting box or crosshairs to be as small as possible when aiming your weapon. This can be achieved by standing still, crouching down, and pressing the Aim button for the weapon before pulling the trigger. Notice the same targeting crosshair on the wall (from the same weapon) is now very small because the soldier is crouching down and not moving.

The shooting accuracy of virtually all guns available on the island improves dramatically when your soldier is standing still, as opposed to walking, running, jumping, or moving when aiming the weapon.

Depending on the weapon, there are several ways to aim and then fire it. When any gun is active, point it toward your enemy and pull the trigger to fire it. This strategy works well when you're in close range, when time is more important than aiming accuracy because you're close to the enemy and it'll be difficult to miss your intended target. This is referred to as "shooting from the hip."

By pressing the Aim button before pulling the trigger, you'll achieve more accurate aim for the weapon you're using, particularly if your soldier is crouching or standing still.

Anytime you're using a weapon with a built-in scope, pressing the Aim button activates the scope and changes your view. The farther you are from your target, the more you may need to compensate for bullet drop, so aim slightly higher than your intended target. Learning to accurately account for bullet drop takes practice, and the technique varies for each type of long-range weapon.

The aiming process for throwable weapons (such as Grenades) is different than shooting a gun. Notice the targeting crosshairs look different. When you toss a Grenade, it follows an arc-like trajectory. In some cases, if you're trying to toss a Grenade through a small open window of a building or fortress, it may be necessary to aim slightly higher than your intended target. Shown here, several Grenades were tossed through the window of this house from a distance. As a result, the inside of the house was blown up and gutted. Anyone inside would literally be toast.

Maintain a Similar Arsenal During Each Match

Unless you have a specific objective in mind, especially during the early stages of a match, you'll be well served by collecting and maintaining a well-balanced arsenal, and then upgrading and tweaking your arsenal as you reach later stages of the match.

A well-rounded arsenal might include an assault rifle, shotgun, sniper rifle (or scoped weapon), an explosive, along with a Health/Shield replenishment item. This combination of weapons and items will allow you to hold your own in close-range, mid-range, or long-range combat situations.

Of course, in conjunction with each weapon, you'll need an ample supply of ammo. As you explore the island, take time to open Ammo Boxes as a way to increase your ammo supply and stock up on harder-to-find ammo types, like Rockets.

Early on, if all you can find is a Pistol, of course grab it (if it's the only weapon you can initially find), but then replace it within your soldier's inventory as soon as something better comes along. Then once you've acquired a well-rounded arsenal, look to improve it by collecting or upgrading weapons to higher rankings. In a perfect situation, you'll have all Legendary ranked weapons as you enter into an End Game.

Like weapons, ammo can also be acquired by finding it lying out in the open (on the ground); by opening chests, Loot Llamas, and Supply Drops; and by defeating enemies and taking what they leave behind.

Every Gun Has a Unique Reload Time and Magazine Size

As you'll see by viewing information about the weapons your soldier is carrying from the Backpack Inventory screen, every type of gun in Fortnite: Battle Royale *has a specific Magazine Size, which determines how many bullets it can hold at once. Each gun also has a pre-determined number of shots it can fire per second, whether you quickly press and release the trigger or hold down the trigger. Once you've used up all of the ammo within the gun's magazine, it's necessary to reload the weapon. How long this reload process takes varies greatly, depending on the weapon.*

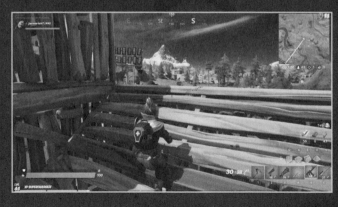

During those few seconds a weapon is reloading (assuming your soldier is carrying enough compatible ammunition to reload that weapon), your soldier will be vulnerable. It's best to crouch down (to make your soldier a smaller target) and then hide behind a solid object during the reload process.

Depending on the weapon, instead of waiting for a weapon to reload, it's sometimes faster to switch to a different fully loaded weapon that's already in your soldier's arsenal. Get to know the reload time for the various weapons you'll be using, so during an intense combat situation, you can quickly determine whether it's safer and more efficient to reload the weapon your soldier is using or switch to a different weapon.

If you've become highly proficient using a specific type of weapon that you know has a long reload time, consider collecting two identical weapons and storing them side-by-side within your soldier's inventory. This way, instead of waiting for the one weapon to reload, you can quickly switch to the other. Notice that the two inventory slots on the right both contain a Sniper Rifle. Since the Magazine Size of this weapon is small, and the Reload Time is long, it's often faster to switch between these two identical weapons.

Ways to Attack a Moving Vehicle (Such as a Speed Boat)

Always listen for the sound of an approaching vehicle. You'll often hear it coming closer before you can see it. Once you spot an enemy driving a vehicle, you have four options:

- Use your gun and start shooting. You can either aim for the driver and try to defeat them directly or aim for the vehicle and inflict as much HP damage as possible. From a distance, using a Sniper Rifle (or weapon with a scope) works nicely, but you need to take into account that the vehicle is in motion, and aim accordingly. In other words, depending on your distance from the vehicle, aim slightly in front of it.

- Attack a vehicle using throwable explosives. If the Grenade, for example, hits the outside of a vehicle, it'll often just bounce off.
- Take advantage of a projectile exploding weapon. Target the vehicle and blast it with one or two direct hits. This strategy will typically defeat (or at least injure) whomever is inside the vehicle.
- Avoid the vehicle altogether and allow it to pass without a confrontation.

Responsibilities You'll Need to Juggle When It Comes to Combat

When it comes to working with weapons during a match, you'll consistently need to use six essential skills, including:

1. Finding weapons and then adding the best selection of them to your soldier's arsenal. The weapons you collect get stored within your soldier's backpack. It only has slots for up to six weapons and/or loot items (excluding your soldier's Harvesting Tool, which can also be used as a short-range weapon).
2. Choosing the most appropriate weapon based on each combat situation. This means quickly analyzing the challenges and rivals you're currently facing, and selecting a close-range, mid-range, or long-range gun, an explosive weapon, or

a projectile explosive weapon that'll help you get the current job done.
3. Collecting and stockpiling the different types of ammunition and making sure you have an ample supply of ammunition for each weapon you want to use.
4. Positioning yourself in the ideal location, with direct line-of-sight to your target(s), so you can inflict damage in the most accurate and efficient way possible. Headshots always cause more damage than a body shot, for example, when targeting enemies.
5. Aiming each type of weapon, so you're able to consistently hit your targets, without wasting ammunition or increasing the risk of your enemies having time to shoot back. When your soldier crouches down while shooting a weapon, their aim will always improve.
6. Shooting the active weapon your soldier is holding, and then quickly switching between weapons as needed. You'll also need to take cover each time a weapon needs to be reloaded.

Once you get good at performing each of these tasks, it'll still take a lot of practice to become a highly skilled sharpshooter who is capable of using single shots to defeat enemies. Plus, you'll need to discover how to best use the weapons at your disposal to destroy structures and fortresses in which your enemies may be hiding.

Collecting and Using Resources

Wood, stone, and metal are the three resources available on the island. Each can be used to build with or used to upgrade your weapons when you approach a Weapon Upgrade Bench.

When it comes to building, wood is the weakest material, but also the fastest to work with. Use wood to build ramps and bridges. Structures made from wood can easily be destroyed or damaged by enemy attacks or explosions.

Stone is stronger than wood and takes a bit longer to build with. Use stone to build defensive structures when metal isn't available, or you need the structure to be completed quickly in order to defend your position.

Keep in mind, in a combat situation when you need to protect your soldier, even the simplest structures can be extremely useful and they can be built very quickly. Anytime you're building a multi-level structure, be sure to create a strong base on the ground level to ensure the structure will be sturdy.

As you'll discover in the section called *Building Strategies & Techniques*, there are four main building tile shapes you can work with to create all sorts of buildings, structures, ramps, and bridges. These include Wall Tiles, Floor/Ceiling Tiles, Ramp/Stair Tiles, and Pyramid-Shaped Tiles.

Metal is the strongest material to build with, but your construction will take longer to complete. Remember, while building tiles are being constructed, each tile's HP strength slowly increases. A tile does not reach its full HP capacity until it's fully built.

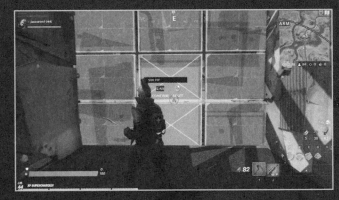

While in Building mode, you can use the game's Editing tools to modify the shape of each core building tile, to give you more creative control when it comes to building any type of structure. For example, you can quickly and easily add windows or doors to wall tiles. Shown here, a door is being added to the metal wall within this small fortress.

Within the same metal fortress, a single window is being added to a wall that's adjacent to the door.

Here's what the window looks like once it's been created by editing the vertical wall tile.

Once structures are built, however, they can easily be damaged as a result on an incoming attack or explosion. When this happens, you have several choices. You can abandon the structure altogether, you can rebuild destroyed tiles from scratch, or you can repair individual building tiles that are damaged (before they get destroyed).

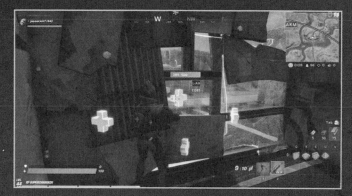

Repairing damaged building tiles requires additional resources. When a building tile gets damaged, it begins to become translucent. At this point, it's HP will be diminished. Once a building tile's HP meter hits zero, that tile will be destroyed. However, if you have your soldier face the tile and use the Repair command, using resources, you can initiate repairs to that tile that take several seconds to complete.

If the tile is receiving continuous incoming fire, depending on the enemy weapon being used, you may not be able to repair that tile faster than the damage is being inflicted. Should you discover this is the case, consider retreating or somehow changing up the structure's design with additional building.

Ways to Harvest Resources

There are several ways to harvest and collect resources. These include:

Use your soldier's Harvesting Tool to smash anything made of wood, such as trees or wooden pallets, to collect wood.

Use your soldier's Harvesting Tool to smash anything made of brick or stone, such as stone piles or brick walls, to collect stone.

Use your soldier's Harvesting tool to smash anything made of metal, such as broken down vehicles, appliances, machinery, or metal structures, to collect metal.

Find, grab, and collect resource icons that are often found out in the open. Each icon is worth a bundle of that resource. Shown here are wood and metal icons. Grab them to collect some extra wood and metal.

Eliminate enemies from the match and then grab the weapons, ammo, loot items, and resources they leave behind. Especially in later stages of a match, a soldier is likely to have amassed a large collection of wood, stone, and metal.

Bundles of resources can also be acquired by opening chests, smashing Loot Llamas, or by finding and opening Supply Drops.

Catch and Consume Fish

In addition to using Health and Shield replenishment items, like Med Kits, Bandages, and Shield Potions, that you're likely already familiar with from past gaming seasons, it's now possible to collect and consume fish in order to boost or replenish your soldier's Health meter.

Fishing rods only work when you cast them into water where you see fish swimming around. After catching one or two fish, you'll likely need to find another fishing spot.

Of course, you'll need to locate and then catch the fish first. To do this, first find and grab a fishing rod, and then approach a body of water where you see fish swimming around.

After you catch a fish, you can grab it and add it to your soldier's inventory. This requires an inventory slot. You can also grab and consume it right away. It takes just one second to consume in order to replenish some of your soldier's Health meter. How much Health HP you receive will depend on the type of fish you catch and consume.

Cast the fishing line into the water, aiming for the fish. When you see a fish nibbling of the hook, reel in the fishing line.

While fishing, in addition to catching fish, you're fishing hook is likely to snag onto weapons and other items that you can reel in, collect, and use as needed.

Anytime you're standing at the edge of a lake, stream, or river doing some fishing, your soldier will theoretically be out in the open and vulnerable to attack. Consider building a small defensive structure around your soldier before you start fishing (don't forget to add a roof) or be ready to quickly switch from the fishing rod to a weapon to return an incoming attack when necessary.

During your fishing expeditions, the type of fish you really want to catch is the much-sought-after and extremely rare Mythic Goldfish. This type of fish can be used as a weapon to seriously injure enemies or utterly destroy a structure, for example, so use it wisely.

Building Strategies & Techniques

Learning to quickly build during a match is a separate skillset you'll want to master. While in Building mode, your soldier can use different-shaped building tiles to construct structures and fortresses. To be able to build, your soldier must first collect and harvest resources, including wood, stone, and metal.

There are four different building tile shapes you can work with, including: horizontal floor/ceiling tiles, vertical wall tiles, ramp/stair-shaped tiles, and pyramid-shaped tiles. Each tile type can be constructed using wood, stone, or metal. Mix and match the building tiles to create custom-designed structures and fortresses.

The following chart shows the maximum HP for each type of building tile you can work with. Keep in mind, Epic Games has tweaked this information multiple times in the past, so when you play *Fortnite: Battle Royale*, the HP strength of each tile may vary.

TILE SHAPE	WOOD	STONE	METAL
Horizontal Floor/Ceiling Tile	140 HP	280 HP	460 HP
Vertical Wall Tile	150 HP	300 HP	500 HP
Ramp/Stairs Tile	140 HP	280 HP	460 HP
Pyramid-Shaped Tile	140 HP	280 HP	460 HP

Here, from left to right, the vertical wall tiles have been constructed from wood, stone, and metal, respectively.

When a ramp/stair-shaped building tile is selected, a ramp is automatically created when wood is used. Stairs are created when either stone or metal is used.

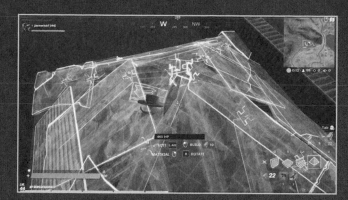

Pyramid-shaped tiles can be used as a roof of a building or structure or placed within a building or structure to provide a protective barrier or additional shielding from incoming attacks. It's also possible to build a pyramid-shaped tile on top of your soldier so they can hide within it for protection. This is a quick and easy way to build a one-tile structure that can block some incoming attacks.

Each building tile has its own HP meter. When that tile's HP meter hits zero, as a result of being damaged from a Harvesting Tool, weapon, or explosive attack, that tile will be destroyed. A soldier has the ability to repair a damaged tile (which requires additional resources). As damage is inflicted on a building tile, it will become translucent and its HP meter will decrease. Several shots have been fired on this metal vertical wall tile. Its HP meter is currently at 234 out of 500. When a tile is translucent (meaning it's been damaged), you can see through it, however, your enemies can see through it from the opposite side as well.

Using the Editing tools available while in Building mode, it's possible to build a window or door, for example, into a vertical or horizontal building tile. When you do this, the maximum HP for that tile will be reduced slightly. By editing a pyramid-shaped tile as it's being built, it's possible to create a lean-to structure using one tile.

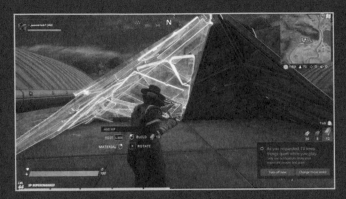

When you place several of these edited pyramid-shaped tiles next to each other, you're able to construct a larger size pyramid, which can be used as a fortress or protective structure.

If your soldier is being shot at and you need to build a quick structure for protection, first build a horizontal wall-shaped tile out of stone or metal. Immediately behind it, build a stairs tile, also out of stone or metal. Your soldier can now crouch down behind the stairs. An incoming attack will first need to go through two building tiles before reaching your soldier. Add walls to protect your soldier from both sides as well.

Displayed below the mini-map on the main game screen is a timer that tells you when the storm will form, or when it will next expand and move. In this case, the storm will expand and move again in 20 seconds.

Beware of the Deadly Storm

As if dealing with up to 99 enemies on the island wasn't enough, within minutes after your soldier's arrival, a deadly storm will form and begin to expand, until it eventually engulfs almost the entire island during the final minutes of a match (when only a few soldiers remain alive).

Within the mini-map, follow the white line to discover the shortest route between your soldier's current location on the island and the next safe zone (which is the area not yet made uninhabitable by the storm).

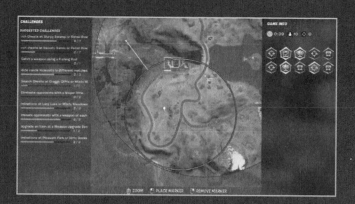

Shown here is the Island Map. In this case, the soldier needs to travel a decent distance to reach the next safe zone.

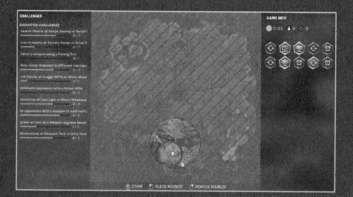

Both within the mini-map, as well as on the Island Map screen, the areas of the island shown in pink have already been made uninhabitable by the storm. Anytime you see two circles displayed on the Island Map, the outer circle in the current safe area, and the inner (smaller) circle shows you where the safe region will be once the deadly storm expands and moves again.

While exploring the island, the edge of the storm is depicted as a blue wall. As long as your soldier stays on the safe side of the blue wall (within the safe zone circle depicted on the map), your biggest concern will be the enemy soldiers remaining on the island who are trying to eliminate your soldier from the match.

For each second your soldier finds himself on the wrong side of the blue wall and caught within the deadly storm, some of their Health meter will be depleted. Once your soldier's Health meter reaches zero, they will immediately be eliminated from the match. If your soldier enters the storm ravaged area during the early stages of the match, the speed that their Health meter will be depleted starts off slow.

Later in the match, your soldier will receive greater damage to their Health meter faster. On most gaming systems, a soldier's Health and Shield meters are displayed near the bottom-center of the screen. Remember, Shields do not protect your soldier from damage caused by the storm.

Take Advantage of the Island Map

When it's safe to do so, check the Island Map. Anytime you do this, however, whatever is happening on the island does not pause, but you won't be able to see what's going on. As you're looking at the map, listen carefully for the sounds of impending danger.

While your soldier is in the pre-deployment area or riding on the Battle Bus, from the Island Map you can see the random route the bus will travel over the island. This information is useful when it comes to choosing your landing spot.

Throughout the rest of each match, the Island Map also offers a lot of information, including:

- You're able to clearly see all of the labeled points of interest on the map.
- Your soldier's current location is displayed on the map as a small, arrow-shaped icon. Different colored icons are used to show you the current location of your partner or squad mates if you're playing a Duos, Squads, or a team-oriented match. The location of your enemies is never displayed on the Island Map.
- The pink area on the map is the area of the island that's already been engulfed by the deadly storm and is uninhabitable.
- The outer circle on the map shows the current safe zone, while the inner circle shows where the safe zone will be once the storm expands and moves again.

- Markers can be placed on the map to help you, your partner, or your squad mates navigate to a specific location on the island.

Markers can be placed on the Island Map. At the start of a match, while you're still in the pre-deployment area, or while riding on the Battle Bus, placing a marker on the map shows your partner or squad mates where you intend to land, and allows you to quickly set a rendezvous location without having to talk. You, as well as your partner or squad mates can all add different colored markers to the Island Map screen, as needed. Shown here, a blue marker has been placed to the immediate right of Frenzy Farm on the Island Map.

Once one or more markers have been placed on the Map Screen, they're displayed as colored flares on the main game screen, and they can be seen from great distances. Even if you're playing a Solo match, when you know you're trying to reach a specific location, placing a marker on the Island Map makes that location easier to see from a distance when you're navigating your way to it.

Preparing for and Surviving the End Game

As the End Game approaches, study the storm's location and movement carefully. There are two distinct strategies gamers use to survive this part of the match, allowing them to potentially achieve #1 Victory Royale.

First, stay in the dead center of the safe zone within the storm as it shrinks down. By staying in the center (preferably on top of a mountain, hill, or structure that gives you a height advantage), you can see enemies approaching from all sides and potentially take them out using a gun or explosive weapon.

An alternate strategy is to stay at the very edge of the safe zone, trying to stay out of sight. You can then pick off enemies moving around near the center of the safe zone, assuming they can be seen out in the open.

As you're forced into closer and closer proximity with the soldiers who remain alive during the final minutes of a match, you'll often be forced to fight. At this point, you can go on the offensive and launch attacks, or you can try to hang back and allow your enemies to fight amongst themselves and eliminate each other while you stay in a safe location and watch, while conserving your ammo and maintaining your soldier's Health and Shield levels.

Then, when only one or two enemies remain, you can launch your own attacks or be in a strong position to defend against incoming attacks from those final enemies. At this point, building will often be necessary to create defensive structures and/or to gain a height advantage.

In fact, once the storm almost fully engulfs the island, those final minutes of a match might take place with you and the remaining enemies within a single structure, literally above or below each other. In these situations, it'll typically be the soldier who has the height advantage, the most powerful weapon, and who reacts the fastest in a shootout who will win the match.

It's always good to enter into an End Game with your soldier's inventory chock full of wood, stone, and metal, so you can build ramps, bridges, protective walls, or entire fortresses, as they're needed. If you manage to make it to the very last moments of a match, and must fight just one or two remaining enemies, you'll need the most powerful close- to mid-range weapons you can get your hands on. You'll also need plenty of compatible ammo, so be sure to stock up beforehand!

At this point in the match, a long-range weapon, a projectile explosive weapon, or any weapon with a scope will no longer be useful, since everyone who is still alive will be forced into very close proximity, thanks to the storm.

Thirteen Additional End Game Strategies

Preparation is the key when you enter into the End Game in hopes of winning a match. It's also important to stay calm, watch what your enemies are doing, and stay focused on your objectives.

1. **Choose the Best Location If You Decide to Build a Fortress—**Based on the terrain where the final safe zone of the island is during the End Game, select the best location to build your fortress, from which you'll likely make your final stand in battle. If you're in a good position, you can be more aggressive with your attacks. If you're in the dead-center of the final circle, your soldier may become the center of attention, which probably isn't good. Make sure your fortress is tall, well-fortified, and that it offers an excellent, 360-degree view of the surrounding area from the top level.

2. **Have a back-up plan—**Should your fortress get destroyed or get engulfed by the storm, be prepared to move quickly, and have a backup strategy in place that will help to ensure your survival. Having the element of surprise for your attacks gives you a tactical advantage. Don't become an easy target to hit. Have your soldier keep moving around within their fort, and while they're out in the open!

3. **During the End Game, Don't Engage Every Remaining Soldier—**Sometimes it makes more sense to conserve your ammo and allow some of the remaining enemies to fight amongst themselves to reduce their

numbers, plus reduce or even deplete their ammo and resources.

4. **Keep Tabs on the Location of Your Enemies—**Don't allow enemies to sneak up behind you (or approach from above), for example, during an End Game. Even if your back is to the storm, an enemy could enter the storm temporarily, and then emerge behind you to launch a surprise attack if you lose track of their location.

5. **Only Build When Necessary—**Don't invest a lot of resources into a massive and highly fortified fortress until you know you're in the final circle during a match. Refer to the map and the displayed timer. Otherwise, when the storm expands and moves, you could find it necessary to abandon your fort, and then need to build another one quickly, in a not-so-ideal location. Having to rebuild will use up your resources. Base pushers are enemies that aren't afraid to leave their fortress and attempt to attack yours during the final minutes of a match. Be prepared to deal with their close-range threat.

6. **Focus on One Enemy at a Time—**If two or three enemies remain, focus on one at a time. Determine who appears to be the most immanent and largest threat. Be prepared to change priorities at a moment's notice, based on the actions of your enemies.

7. **Be Ready to Replenish Your Health and Shields—**Have Health and Shield replenishment items on hand to boost your soldier's Health and Shield meters after your soldier has been attacked. Find a safe place

to hide before using an item that'll take seconds to consume or use, during which time your soldier will be vulnerable.

8. **Prepare for Close-Range Combat—**In some End Game situations, the only recourse is to engage the final enemies in close-range combat. Sometimes, the remaining safe area is so tiny, your enemy will either be directly on top of or below you. Be prepared for this and use weapons that can defeat enemies and/or destroy the structure or object an enemy is standing on or crouching behind.

9. **Be Prepared to Make a Quick Retreat—**Be prepared to make a quick retreat from your current location if you're confronted by an enemy whose arsenal is clearly more powerful than yours, or if your current position is not conducive to achieving a win. For example, if an enemy clearly has a height advantage, you don't have enough ammo on hand to defeat the enemy, or your soldier's Health is dangerously low already.

10. **Shoot at Bushes to Lure Out Enemies Hiding Within Them—**Sometimes, an End Game will take place out in the open. There will be no place to hide and building a structure yourself will quickly reveal your location. In this case, consider hiding within (not behind) a large bush. You'll remain out of sight and can launch an attack if an enemy comes too close. However, savvy gamers know to shoot at bushes during the End Game when they can't locate their enemies.

Bushes offer no protection against bullets or explosives whatsoever. They simply provide a place to hide.

11. **Practice the Art of Ultra-Fast Building—**Some End Games require gamers to quickly build and repair fortresses or structures to gain a height advantage, to provide a place to hide, or for protection against incoming attacks. When your final adversaries are in very close proximity, the soldier who can build (and repair structures) the fastest, achieve a height advantage over their enemy, and then switch to Combat mode to shoot the fastest will almost always win the match. Don't just practice basic building skills. Make sure you're able to build very quickly and are comfortable switching between Building and Combat modes at lightning fast speed during a firefight.

12. **React Fast When You're Face-to-Face with an Enemy—**When it comes down to just you and one or two other enemies during an End Game, the winner of the match will likely be determined based on who reacts the fastest when choosing an appropriate close-range weapon, and which gamer can target their moving enemy the most accurately. Of course, having a height advantage and making sure your soldier has ample Shields to withstand a few bullet hits will be beneficial.

13. **Sometimes It Makes Sense to Just Kick Back and Chill or Do Some Recon—**During the End Game, if you find a safe place to hide, use it.

Allow the other remaining soldiers to fight each other and waste their ammo, while you take a few minutes to relax, replenish your soldier's Health and Shield meters, and think about your next attack strategy. Just make sure when you choose a hiding place that it's well within the safe zone. When the storm expands and moves again, and a few of the soldiers have eliminated each other, you can re-enter the match fully ready to face your next challenge.

Study Your Opponents and Learn from Their Mistakes

Most gamers have a favorite weapon and a strategy that they rely on often. Simply by watching your enemies, you can quickly discover their skill level and determine whether or not you'll be able to defeat them easily in a firefight.

Don't take unnecessary risks, especially early in a match. If you see you're outgunned, or an opponent is clearly more experienced than you, retreat and hide to avoid a confrontation. However, if you sense the enemy is being controlled by a newb, go on the offensive.

Anytime your soldier's arsenal includes a scoped weapon, such as a Sniper Rifle, keep your distance from an enemy. Find a good place to hide that has a clear line of sight to your enemy, and then wait for them to stand still for a second or two so you can get a clear shot.

 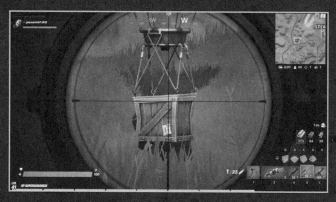

One strategy is to be on the lookout for a nearby chest, Loot Llama, or Supply Drop that you know enemies will approach. Keep your distance and target the object using your scoped weapon. As soon as the enemy moves in to open the chest, Loot Llama, or Supply Drop and appears within your targeting crosshairs (or within your scope), open fire.

Watch the Pros at Work

One of the best ways to learn new strategies is to watch experienced gamers play *Fortnite: Battle Royale*. Thanks to streaming services like Twitch, Mixer, and YouTube, there is no shortage of skilled gamers who regularly broadcast on these services and who publish pre-recorded video content on YouTube.

In addition, once you get eliminated from a match, instead of quickly exiting out and jumping right into a new match, consider sticking around as a spectator. Chances are, the gamers who last until the End Game will be highly skilled, so you can learn from them.

Keep Practicing!

Be realistic! You're not going to become an awesome gamer overnight! Developing the skills you'll need to consistently win matches, and eventually rank highly in competitions, is going to take a lot of practice.

As you're participating in Solo, Duos, and Squad matches when playing *Fortnite: Battle Royale*, focus on boosting your XP level and completing the various challenges/missions required to complete Battle Pass Tiers. These are designed to help you round out and enhance your gaming skills and expose you to different aspects of the game.

In addition, spend time in Playground mode, especially if you need practice working with weapons and building. You can hone your combat skills as well by participating in team-oriented matches, since your soldier will typically be able to respawn numerous times during each team-oriented match, so you don't have to worry too much about being eliminated, and can focus more on working with weapons, building, working with team-mates, and confronting enemies in a wide range of combat situations and locations.

No matter how much you "study" *Fortnite: Battle Royale*, once you've memorized the layout of the terrain and got acquainted with all of the weapons, ammo types, loot items, tools, and vehicles at your disposal, the way to become a highly skilled and successful gamer is to keep practicing!

SECTION 4

HOW TO TAKE YOUR GAMING TO THE PRO LEVEL

The first step to becoming a "pro" *Fortnite* gamer is to master your combat, exploration, survival, and building skills to the point where you're consistently achieving #1 Victory Royale when playing the various game play modes in *Fortnite: Battle Royale*. This alone is going to take a lot of practice. There are more than 250 million registered *Fortnite: Battle Royale* gamers around the world, so you can expect to encounter a ton of fierce competition!

The next step toward becoming a pro is to upgrade your gaming gear. (Refer back to *Section 2, Upgrade Your Gaming Gear to Pro Level* for more information on what this entails.) Ultimately, once you start qualifying for Tournaments, you'll likely be expected to play *Fortnite: Battle Royale* on a souped-up Windows PC that's equipped with a pro-quality gaming keyboard, high-end monitor, gaming mouse, and a gaming headset, not to mention a powerful CPU and graphics card. Don't worry, once you start winning competitions and building a following of fans, you could get sponsored and/or be recruited onto an eSports team, so you won't necessarily have to pay for the required gaming gear yourself.

What It Means to Be a Pro *Fortnite* Gamer

The third step toward becoming a pro is to begin participating in Epic Games' various specialty game play modes that allow you to qualify for its officially sanctioned competitions and Tournaments. This is something you can start doing right away! How to do this will be explained shortly.

Throughout the year, Epic Games hosts an ongoing series of in-game competitions and invitation-only competitive events and Tournaments that are held around the world. The majority of these competitions award cash prizes to the top-ranked and winning players.

When you start winning competitions, and you're earning money from prizes, sponsorships, and from your online viewership, this means you've become a pro gamer. At this point, playing *Fortnite: Battle Royale* is no longer something you just do for fun. You're expected to play at least six to twelve hours per day, since it's now your full-time job!

The *Fortnite World Cup* Awaits the Best of the Best Gamers

In July 2019, the world's first *Fortnite World Cup* competition was held in New York City. More than 40 million players tried to qualify for this multi-day event, which was attended by more than 19,000 *Fortnite* fans and was watched live by more than 2.3 million viewers on YouTube and Twitch. At the time, this was the most watched competitive gaming event ever held anywhere in the world (excluding China).

The second annual *Fortnite World Cup* will no doubt be even more successful, and more players will quickly become household names as they take home millions of dollars in prize money.

Before you consider "going pro," even if you think you have the gaming skills required to succeed, tune in and watch some of the live competitions and Tournaments that Epic Games hosts. They're streamed live on Twitch, YouTube, and Fortnite.com/watch, plus you can watch past competitions on-demand. This is your chance to scope out the potential competition, and in your mind, figure out if you're actually worthy to compete and have the mental wherewithal to deal with the intense pressure of competition.

- **To watch a replay of the 2019 Creative Finals + Pro-Am on YouTube, visit: www.youtube.com/ watch?v=Gkrsn3k2u9s**
- **To watch the 2019 *Fortnite World Cup* Solo Finals on YouTube, visit: https://www.youtube.com/ watch?v=2xG1Umugpxs**
- **To watch the 2019 *Fortnite World Cup* Duos Finals on YouTube, visit: www. youtube.com/watch?v=31HqRnWrg3Y**

Discover what it's like participating in the Fortnite World Cup *by watching a replay of the 2019 competition's various online broadcasts. As you can see here, the* Fortnite World Cup *Finals– Day 3 video on YouTube has already been watched by more than 13.3 million gamers.*

The official Epic Games website is one place to visit in order to discover the latest details about upcoming Fortnite World Cup *competitions (and officially sanctioned Tournaments leading up to this mega-event). Point your web browser to: www.epicgames. com/fortnite/competitive/en-US/events/world-cup.*

Of course, simply thinking you could be the next Kyle "Bugha" Giersdorf (@bugha) and take home the *Fortnite World Cup* Solos Winner title and $3 million (US) is one thing. Being able to prove it is another thing altogether. Long before you earn a place in the next annual *Fortnite World Cup*, you'll need to qualify and become a top-ranked player in a variety of officially sanctioned online events and regional tournaments.

Participate in Epic Games, Sanctioned Competitions & Events

To discover which game play modes you'll need to master to qualify for a spot in an upcoming Tournament, from the Fortnite: Battle Royale *Lobby, click on the Compete tab that's located at the top-center of the screen.*

When details about a specific Event are displayed, click on the **Tournament Details** *button to determine if you could qualify and learn how to participate.*

Next, select a current or upcoming Event from the menu. Click on the Event Details button associated with a specific Event to see more information.

Some information about current and upcoming competitions is displayed within the game. New Events are hosted each week.

For complete details about Epic Games Events, visit:

- www.epicgames.com/fortnite/competitive/en-US/home
- www.epicgames.com/fortnite/competitive/en-US/news
- www.epicgames.com/fortnite/competitive/en-US/events#event-guidelines

Each gaming season, Epic Games now offers upwards of $100,000,000 (US) in prize money. Following the very first *Fortnite World Cup* that was held in July 2019 during *Fortnite: Battle Royale*'s Season X, for example, the company hosted the *Fortnite Champion Series*.

A player's quest to win some of the cash that was up for grabs during the *Fortnite Champion Series* began when a gamer reached the "Champion League" level while playing Arena mode. Only then could that player qualify to participate in the three Tournament Rounds that were held over a five-week period.

Round One (Opens) in the Tournament Rounds of the *Fortnite Champion Series* took all who qualified and whittled down this large group dramatically. Round Two accepted only the top 1,000 ranked gamers per region. Round three narrowed down the competition yet again to just 150 of the top ranked competitors. Then the top eight teams from Round Three from each region were given the chance to advance to the Season Finals. After this extremely competitive Tournament, the elite Season X Champions were crowned.

Season Final winners could advance even further, working their way toward a 2020 *Fortnite World Cup* invitation, which would again offer more than $30 million in cash prizes. Meanwhile, for those who didn't qualify to participate in the *Fortnite Champion Series*, throughout Season X Epic Games hosted a series of what it called "smaller Tournaments" each week. Several of these in-game, one-day Tournaments were called Cash Cups.

During Chapter 2, Season 1 and beyond, the weekly, in-game Tournaments continued. Each required gamers to become a top-ranked player in a specific *Fortnite: Battle Royale* game play mode (such as Arenas), or while playing a specific map created using *Fortnite: Creative*.

In addition, beyond the officially sanctioned and Epic Games–hosted Tournaments taking place throughout each gaming season, through the *Fortnite* Spotlight program, independent, user-run events, tournaments, and competitions that meet Epic Games' guidelines continue to be hosted online and around the world, giving gamers even more opportunities to shine as an up-and-coming pro gamer.

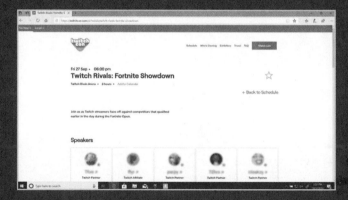

And then there are Fortnite: Battle Royale *competitions and tournaments hosted by services like Twitch. At TwitchCon 2019 in San Diego, for example, the* Fortnite Twitch Open *(https://twitchcon.com/schedule/fortnite-open) was held in late-September 2019. It allowed participants to earn a spot in the* Fortnite Twitch Showdown *(https://twitchcon.com/schedule/fortnite-showdown), which is likely to become an annual event.*

Consider Joining an eSports Team

If your goal is to join a top-ranked *Fortnite* eSports team that regularly competes on a regional, national, or international level, you'll need to be recruited. The way to help make this happen is simply to start participating in Competitions, Cash Cups, and Tournaments within the game, consistently achieve a high ranking, and capture the attention of team managers or organizers.

As you're working your way up to being recruited onto a high-profile, professional team, consider joining an independent team comprised of gamers at your skill and experience level. One online tool that can help you find team members and establish your own team (or introduce you to already established teams looking for new members) is called Axon (www.axon.gg).

Begin by setting up a free Axon account and creating a profile for yourself. Your profile should include your photo, gaming name, a short bio, your location, a listing of games you're really good at (including *Fortnite: Battle Royale*), video clips of your finest moments playing those games, and links to your social media accounts, YouTube channel, and any other gaming networks (such as Twitch or Mixer) you're part of.

After creating a profile, use the Axon website to browse listings for thousands of independent teams looking for members. Alternatively, click on the Create a Team button to establish your own team, and then search the service's Players database to browse through profiles and seek out potential members. You're then able to communicate with team leaders or other players using Axon's Messenger service.

Participate in Non-Sanctioned Competitions

Both online and in the real world, there are countless independent *Fortnite: Battle Royale* tournaments anyone is able to compete in and potentially win cash prizes, while at the same time, boosting their reputation as an up-and-coming pro *Fortnite* gamer.

Keep in mind, depending on where you live, some states within the United States, for example, have banned online game competitions that have cash prizes, and most have a minimum age requirement to participate.

To help you discover tournaments and competitions to participate in, enter the search phrase "Online Fortnite Tournaments" into your favorite search engine, such as Google, Yahoo!, or Bing. The following is information about a few of the online services and independent websites you'll likely stumble upon.

One service that hosts regularly scheduled, online-based Fortnite: Battle Royale tournaments for gamers age 16 and up is called GamerzArena (www.gamerzarena.com). Participating in tournaments organized by GamerzArena is free, but a Twitch account is also required, and you must be willing to stream your competitive gameplay live. Each competition has its own set of rules, so be sure you read and understand them before signing up to avoid getting disqualified.

The Players' Lounge (https://playerslounge.co/games) regularly hosts online-based Fortnite: Battle Royale competitions for gamers age 18 and up. From the Choose a Game screen, click on the Join Lounge option associated with the Fortnite listing. Next, select your gaming platform. Options include: PS4 Controller, PS4 Keyboard/Mouse, Xbox One Controller, Xbox One Keyboard/ Mouse, and PC.

From the GamerzArena website, to discover what contests are open, click on the Arena option displayed near the top-left corner of the browser window. From below the Games heading, click on the *Fortnite: Battle Royale* listing by clicking on the Select button. You'll see a listing of contests, including a description of each and how much prize money is at stake. If there's an entry fee, this will be listed as well. Once you discover a contest you wish to compete in, simply click on the Enter Now button.

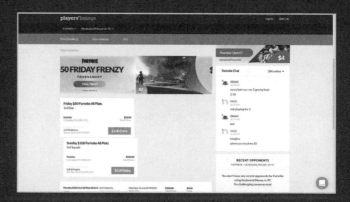

A listing of available Players' Lounge tournaments, their respective entry fees (typically between $1.00 and $5.00) each, and the available prize money (which could be $100.00 or more per competition) is listed. Read the details related to competitions you're interested in, and after setting up a Players' Lounge account, join the tournaments that you want to compete in. As always, be sure to read the Tournament Rules and Game Rules carefully before entering a competition.

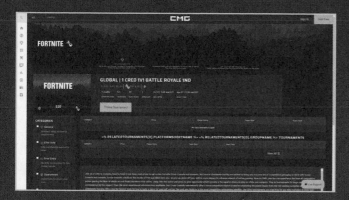

The Checkmate Gaming Network (www.checkmategaming.com) also hosts independent, online-based Fortnite Solo, Duos, and Squads competitions with cash prizes ranging from a few dollars to several hundred dollars per match. To see a listing of Fortnite competitions currently being hosted by this service, visit: www.checkmategaming.com/wager/cross-console/fortnite-battle-royal.

All-Stars eSports League (www.allstarsports.com) is a free-to-join eSports league specifically for high school students in all 50 U.S. states. More than $1 million in annual prize money is offered, and competitions are available to gamers at all skill levels. Each season of gaming competitions last between six and eight weeks. During the regular season, students compete online for a chance to participate in the organization's on-site Regional Championships. Those winners are then invited to participate in the on-site National Championship event for a grand prize.

In addition to individual competitions, The Checkmate Gaming Network hosts bracketed tournaments with larger cash prizes. An entry fee (paid for using credits) is required for each competition you register for. The cost per entry typically varies from between one and five credits.

Credits can be purchased separately for $1.00 (US) each, but you'll save money by purchasing bundles of 5 ($3.75 US), 10 ($7.50 US), 25 ($18.85 US), 50 ($37.50 US), or 100 ($75.00 US) credits. In addition to competing as a solo player, The Checkmate Gaming Network supports eSports teams. If you're looking to join or form a team, be sure to click on the Free Agent menu option.

If you're looking to compete in online tournaments and potentially win cash prizes, some of the other services to check out include:

- **GameBattles**—https://gamebattles.majorleaguegaming.com/ps4/fortnite-cross-play/tournament
- **Glory4Gamers**—https://eu.glory4gamers.com/en/tournaments/ps4/fortnite
- **ProPlayers.eu**—https://proplayers.eu/en
- **UMG Online**—https://umggaming.com/games/fortnite
- **WoDuels**—https://woduels.com/en/game/fortnite

Along with online-based tournaments, a handful of independent promoters are hosting on-site (real world) *Fortnite* competitions in 2020 and beyond. Some of these tournaments are offering more than $250,000 (US) in prize money. For example, DreamHack (https://dreamhack.com) has high-stakes competitions throughout 2020 slated to take place in locations like Anaheim, California and Leipzig, German.

Intel Game Night: *Fortnite* Fridays (https://smash.gg/league/intel-game-night-fortnite-fridays/details) includes competitions held at Microsoft Stores throughout the United States. To find a participating store visit: www.microsoft.com/en-us/store/locations/find-a-store. Weekly prizes include Microsoft Store Gift Cards.

Join the Support-A-Creator Program

Yet another way to earn money as a *Fortnite: Battle Royale* gamer is to join Epic Games' Support-A-Creator program. To do this, you'll first need to amass at least 1,000 followers on one of the supported online streaming or social media services. Once you've accomplished this, simply fill out an application by visiting: www.epicgames.com/affiliate/en-US/overview.

Joining the Support-A-Creator program offers three main perks. First, when followers support you by entering your unique code when playing *Fortnite*, you'll earn $5.00 (US) for every 10,000 V-Bucks they purchase and use within the game.

Second, you're able to use *Fortnite: Creative* to design your own maps and challenges, and then share them with the public by promoting your unique map codes.

Third, you're able to submit your *Fortnite: Creative* submissions to Epic Games, to have them potentially featured within the game itself. Before submitting your work, however, be sure it meets Epic Games' strict guidelines, which can be found online at: http://fortnite.com/news/featured-island-guidelines. To submit your work, follow the directions and link provided on this webpage: www.epicgames.com/fortnite/en-US/news/creative-featured-content.

Other Ways to Earn Money as a *Fortnite* Gamer

Becoming a social media influencer and building up a large audience on a *Fortnite* or game-related YouTube channel, or streaming content live on YouTube Live, Twitch, or Mixer, for example, all offer the potential for earning money from views, sponsorships, merch sales, and advertising revenue, for example.

While becoming a social media influencer can be fun and rewarding, it also requires a major ongoing time commitment. Realistically, it could take you months or potentially years to build up a large enough audience of dedicated viewers or subscribers so you can actually earn money from your efforts. Thus, this is not a get-rich-quick opportunity, or one that's suitable for all gamers. To learn more about what's involved in starting a YouTube channel or becoming a live streamer on a popular game streaming service, be sure to check out the next Section of this guide.

SECTION 5

HOW TO BECOME A *FORTNITE: BATTLE ROYALE* STREAMER AND BUILD YOUR AUDIENCE

When YouTube launched in February 2005 and was then purchased by Google in November 2006, this video streaming service not only changed how people from around the world shared video content via the Internet, it also created an entirely new form of entertainer—known as the *YouTuber*.

Today, YouTubers are also known as *social media influencers*, *content creators*, or *online personalities*. Some have become more famous than A-list television and movie celebrities, chart-topping recording artists, and professional athletes. Using little more than the camera built into their smartphone, the camera built into a computer, or a stand-alone digital camera, a YouTuber is able to record video content from virtually anywhere, edit it, and then quickly share it with the world.

Over time, as YouTubers gained popularity and grew audiences into the millions (and in some cases tens of millions), Google introduced ways for content creators to get paid for their efforts, based on their video views and the loyalty of their audiences. These same online personalities also discovered other ways to earn money from their online exploits by selling branded merchandise (like T-shirts and hoodies), landing their own sponsorships and paid advertisers, and making paid in-person appearances.

YouTubers are able to create pre-recorded video content about almost anything, but some have discovered tremendous success by establishing a gaming-oriented channel and posting videos related to their favorite games, including *Fortnite: Battle Royale*, *Fortnite: Creative*, and/or *Fortnite: Save the World*.

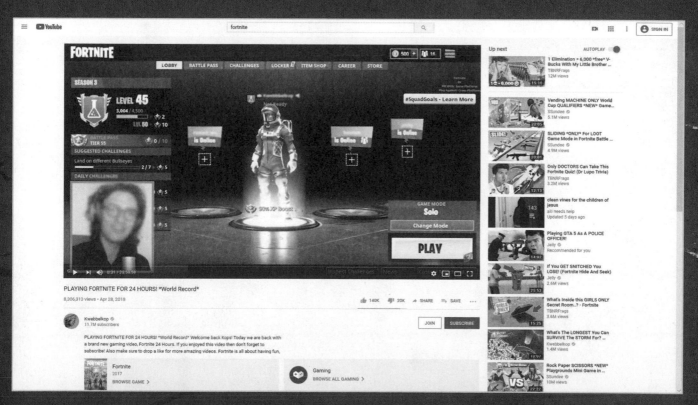

While not a champion gamer who competes in tournaments, Kwebbelkop (www.youtube.com/user/kwebbelkop) is one of many YouTubers who regularly posts popular content related to Fortnite. He has almost 12 million subscribers to his channel (which he established in April 2008). This particular video already has 8.3 million views.

In more recent years, along with publishing pre-recorded and edited video content on YouTube, a variety of online services have made is easy and fun for social media influencers to broadcast and stream live via the Internet.

Many gamers picked up on this fast-growing trend and started offering live streams of themselves playing popular games. As a result, services like Twitch, Mixer, and YouTube Live were born, while popular social media services like Facebook and Instagram also introduced ways for content creators to broadcast live via the Internet—and potentially earn money while building up a vast audience made up of fellow gamers.

Check out Nomxs broadcasting on Twitch as he plays Fortnite: Battle Royale. *Access his Twitch channel by visiting www.twitch.tv/ nomxs. As a highly skilled gamer, people watch his live streams to learn new strategies and see him win many of the matches he participates in.*

Even if your gaming skill hasn't allowed you to win tournaments and competitions, many gamers, just like you, continue to earn money and have fun as social media influencers and content creators by offering game-related content that others enjoy.

Game-Related Videos and Streams Have Many Focuses

Sure, millions of gamers from all over the world turn to YouTube, Twitch, Mixer, and other social media and video streaming services to watch their favorite *Fortnite* players win matches and showcase their skills. In fact, simply watching other highly skilled gamers play *Fortnite* is one of the best ways to learn new strategies, get to know the mysterious island's layout, and discover how to use the latest weapons introduced into the game, for example.

During each of his live broadcasts on Mixer, Ninja typically attracts around 10,000 viewers who watch him play Fortnite: Battle Royale *while he talks to his viewers and responds to their comments and questions. When Ninja isn't broadcasting live (which he typically does several hours per day), replays of his live broadcasts are available for anyone to watch anytime on-demand.*

As you'll discover, some of the more creative content creators showcase a lot more than just their gaming skills in their videos and during their live broadcasts. It's this wide range of *Fortnite*-related content that has allowed so many online personalities and gamers to build large and dedicated audiences and earn money in the process.

In fact, if you look at the videos and live content from well-known *Fortnite* content creators, like Ninja, McCreamy, Kiwiz, Vikkstar123, Bugha, Ali-A, LazarBeam, Nomxs, Myth, and JDuth, for example, you'll quickly discover that while all are highly skilled gamers, each creates vastly different content that showcases their unique personality, gaming skills, creativity, and interests in ways that are highly entertaining and engaging for their respective audiences.

Among his almost 12 million YouTube subscribers, LazarBeam is known for creating very funny and entertaining content, along with reaction videos related to Fortnite: Battle Royale *updates and patches. He's also a pro at creating* Fortnite *memes.*

Thanks to the tools and resources offered by YouTube, Twitch, Mixer, and other services, combined with functionality built directly into *Fortnite*, it's never been easier to record and broadcast game-related content online. Hence, if you choose to become an online personality who specializes in gaming or *Fortnite* specifically, you'll have a lot of competition!

Realistically, you'll need to create new, regularly published content that's informative, creative, original, entertaining, engaging, well-branded, and highly targeted to your intended audience. Only then will you be able to stand out and gain viewers, subscribers, and loyal followers.

Understand right from the start that to achieve online fame, you'll need to publish content or stream live on a regular basis—at least once per week, often more often—and you'll need to stick to a schedule. If you promise your audience a new YouTube video every Wednesday afternoon at 3:00 pm (EST), that new video better be published online and available to your audience every week at that time. Online audiences don't tolerate laziness, excuses, or boring, repetitive content. As soon as you lose peoples' attention, they will simply begin watching, following, and/or subscribing to other peoples' content and streams. As a result, your audience will dwindle quickly.

For the first weeks or months that you begin publishing videos on your own YouTube channel or streaming live on one or more services, chances are your audience will be very small. Even if you do everything correctly, it will likely take weeks or months to build up an audience in the thousands, and potentially several years to grow your audience into the hundreds of thousands or millions.

Keep in mind, while someone like Ninja now has more than 22.5 million subscribers on YouTube alone, he first started his YouTube channel on November 10, 2011. It's taken him eight years and a lot of hard work to achieve his level of popularity online.

Meanwhile, Australian YouTuber and gamer LazarBeam, for example, currently has about 12 million subscribers to his YouTube Channel, but it took him nearly five years of producing content on a regular schedule to achieve his success. You'll need to be both persistent and patient if you want to transform being an online personality into a full-time, money-making job, as opposed to a hobby you do occasionally for fun.

What It Takes to Create Really Good Game-Oriented Content

Out of the thousands of gamers and *Fortnite* enthusiasts who have their own YouTube channels or who stream live on services like Twitch or Mixer, only a small percentage of those people stand out, build up a massive audience, and earn a lot of money.

Here's a Top 10 checklist of what helps the successful content creators stand out from their competition and ultimately build (and keep) their respective audiences:

1. They create/publish highly original, informative, and entertaining content that focuses on a specific topic, such as gaming or Fortnite specifically.
2. Their content is published or streamed on a consistent schedule, so fans know what to expect and when.
3. Their content is original, unique, and extremely creative. In other words, the content creator doesn't just copy other peoples' videos or content because it's trending.
4. Each video or live stream is targeted to a very specific (niche) audience. The audience is made up of people with a specific interest, such as Fortnite, and often who fall into a specific age category (such as gamers between the ages of 8 and 15, ages 15 to 18, or ages 10 and up). Instead of just creating general Fortnite content, however, each creator's content tends to be highly focused. For

example, one YouTuber might create content that exclusively includes Fortnite: Battle Royale Solo game play mode strategies, while someone else might regularly explore new points of interest on the island map, showcase the latest weapons added to the game, offer tips specifically for newbs, or embark on challenges trying to beat Fortnite: Creative Death Run maps. Reaction videos related to each new game update also tend to be popular, assuming as a gamer you have something relevant to say or share.

5. All of the content from each online personality is well-branded. The most "famous" gamers and online personalities have unique nicknames (like Ninja or LazarBeam), as well as their own logo and appearance. It's hard to ignore Ninja's hair color, for example.
6. Each live stream or video is well-produced and looks professional from a visual and sound standpoint. This means having good lighting, a nice background, the right equipment for streaming Fortnite, and a good-quality microphone to capture clear sound.
7. All of the popular content creators showcase their unique personality. People don't just watch videos or live streams for the content. They want to be entertained and get to know the people creating the videos or hosting the live streams. For example, LazarBeam's YouTube videos aren't just informative, they're extremely funny. Each video showcase's

LazarBeam's sense of humor and quirky personality. He continuously makes his audience laugh. When it comes to live streaming, you'll need to be able to successfully play Fortnite: Battle Royal while simultaneously speaking with your audience and responding to their comments and questions, for example.

8. While gamers will watch a really good player's live streams for hours at a time, assuming that streamer is fun and engaging to watch and they're consistently winning Fortnite matches, when it comes to watching pre-recorded videos, audience members have a really short attention span. The best YouTubers create videos that are short (less than three to five minutes each), but that are jam-packed with useful information.

9. Videos that are pre-recorded need to be well edited. As any YouTuber will tell you, editing videos is very time consuming. However, the best videos (and typically the ones that get the most views, likes, shares, and comments), are very well edited and expertly produced. They have short, attention-grabbing, and descriptive titles that don't use clickbait to get noticed. When appropriate, the video's gaming clips are perfectly edited to showcase specific moments that happened during a match. Capturing and recording those game moments also takes a lot of time, patience, and preplanning.

10. The YouTubers and live streamers interact with their audience on a regular basis through comments, multiple social media platforms, or by speaking with them directly and individually during live streams. The goal is to create an online community where online fans communicate with the online personality and with each other, as opposed to just watching videos or live streams passively. Engagement is a major ingredient to every social media influencer's success!

Why Become a Streamer?

There are many reasons why people opt to become YouTubers or online personalities. Some like to showcase their superior gaming skills and want lots of people to see them consistently win *Fortnite: Battle Royale* matches. Others want to share their gaming expertise with others by offering tutorials and how-to content.

Another popular type of game-related video includes reactions to new game updates, or opinion videos. For example, a video topic might be, "My Five Favorite Weapons in *Fortnite*," "Preview of the Newest *Fortnite* Island Locations," "Why I Hate [Insert Something Related to *Fortnite*]" or "What I Love About [Insert Something Related to *Fortnite*]." This type of content requires less gaming skill, but the content creator must have strong options and a good personality. Of course, some people have a huge ego and just want to become online-famous doing whatever antics that'll get them attention and viewers.

One of the biggest reasons why many gamers opt to invest the time and energy to become a YouTuber or online personality is to transform their gaming hobby into a viable money-making opportunity.

Sure, only a very small percentage of gamers actually get rich from their YouTube channel or by streaming on Twitch or Mixer, for example. However, many are able to earn enough money to upgrade their gaming equipment with the latest and greatest hardware, even though their gaming skill level isn't quite good enough for them to consistently win tournaments or contests. Many are also able to earn enough money to forego needing a traditional part-time job to earn extra money.

Whatever your reason for launching a game-related YouTube channel, or becoming a streamer on one of the popular services, understand right from the start that while you'll likely have a lot of fun and meet all sorts of interesting people from around the world, it's going to take a lot of very hard work. If you're already in school full time, or have a regular job, you'll need to manage your time wisely to be able to juggle all of the new responsibilities and commitments required to achieve success online.

Become Active on Social Media

Whether you opt to produce pre-recorded videos for your own YouTube channel or stream live on the Internet via a popular gaming service like Twitch or Mixer, if you want to build a large and dedicated audience of subscribers and followers, you'll also need to become very active on other social media platforms, like Instagram, Twitter, Facebook, Snapchat, and/or TikTok, for example.

Which social media platforms you should become active on will depend on which ones are currently popular with the people who make up the target audience your videos or live streams cater to. Consistently communicating (engaging) with your audience via social media will help you grow your audience and their loyalty, so be prepared to regularly share relevant content on multiple social media platforms.

Of course, you also want to become active on the gaming service related to your gaming hardware, such as the PlayStation Network or Xbox Live Network, and continuously connect with new friends via your Epic Games account while you're playing *Fortnite.*

You're able to manage your Epic Games account, add friends, chat with online friends, and send invitations for online friends to join you for a *Fortnite* match using the ever-improving tools now built into *Fortnite: Battle Royale.*

To access the Social menu while playing Fortnite: Battle Royal, from the Lobby, click on the Social icon that's displayed in the top-left corner of the screen.

The left-most third of the screen will be replaced by the Social menu (shown here). Click on the gear-shaped icon to adjust your Online Status (which other people can see) as well as the Party Privacy option. This can be seen in the top-left area of the screen.

Based on your Epic Games Friends who are currently online and playing Fortnite, use the tools available by clicking on the Party Up button to find and add a Partner for a Duos match, or up to three other gamers to make up your Squad for a Squads match.

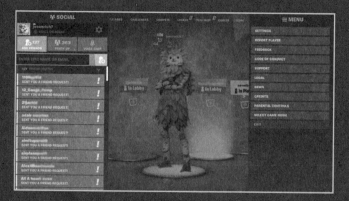

To add friends to your Epic Games account, click on the Add Friends tab (displayed near the top-left corner of the screen) when the Social menu is visible. From here, enter someone's Epic Games account username or email address into the Search field to quickly find and add them as a friend.

To do this, click on a gamer's username. You're then able to send them a Party Invite, give that friend a Nickname, Mute that friend, Remove the friend from your online friends list, or Block the friend if they're being rude, offensive, or annoying.

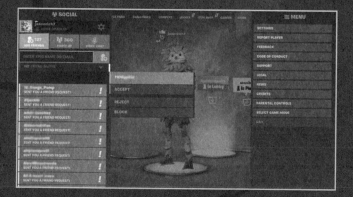

By clicking on a screenname, you're also able to respond to incoming Friend Requests by Accepting, Rejecting, or Blocking each request.

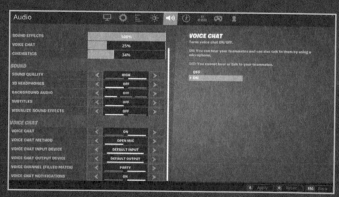

After turning on and adjusting Fortnite's Voice Chat functionality from the game's Audio submenu within Settings, from the Social menu, click on the Voice Chat tab to speak with other online friends while in the Lobby (before actually entering into a match).

Meanwhile, you're able to accept invitations from the Lobby prior to each match. From these incoming invitations, you can select a partner for a Duos match or up three people for a Squads match. Invitations appear as yellow banners that are displayed near soldiers in the center area of the screen.

It's also now possible to use the *Fortnite* mobile app on an iPhone, iPad, or Android-based mobile device to manage online friends linked with your Epic Games account, and to communicate with these friends from within the app (even if you're not playing the mobile version of *Fortnite: Battle Royale* or *Fortnite: Creative*.)

Build Your Brand

What sets online personalities and social media influencers apart is their brand. There are thousands of gamers who regularly publish *Fortnite*-related content, for example. Someone's brand is their overall online identity and persona. It's how people recognize you and relate to you. Your brand also helps to set expectations about what viewers can expect from you and your content.

Your name, personal appearance, reputation, personality, logo, the appearance of your channel, the consistency and creativity of content in your videos (or your live streams) all contribute to your unique brand. Your brand is

something that you need to develop, manage and protect, because it directly relates to your appeal and your ability to attract, maintain, and grow an online audience.

Keep in mind, your brand should appeal to your target audience. Figure out what you're trying to accomplish online, who you want to communicate with, what messages you want to convey, and how you want to present yourself online, then start creating your own personal brand.

If you look at most of the top game-related YouTubers and live streamers, few use their real name. For example, do you have any idea who Richard Tyler Blevins is? You may not know his real name, but as a *Fortnite* fan, you probably know his online name, which is Ninja. Consider coming up with a catchy, memorable, and descriptive name for yourself, as well as a unique and equally catchy channel name.

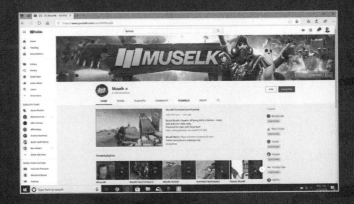

When you visit Muselk's YouTube channel (www.youtube.com/ user/MrMuselk), for example, you'll see his logo continuously displayed on the screen.

When you visit the online store for many popular YouTubers, you'll be able to purchase merchandise, such as T-shirts and hoodies, that feature their logo. Shown here is Lazarbeam's online store (https://shoplazar.com).

Once you've figured out how you want to be known, consider creating a logo for yourself and/or your channel. For help creating a logo, there are a bunch of free or low-cost online tools, such as Wix Logo Maker (www.wix.com/logo/maker), Free Logo Design (www.freelogodesign.org), or Tailor Brands Logo Maker (www.tailorbrands.com/logo-maker).

For between $50.00 and $100.00, another option is to hire a professional graphic designer to help you create a unique logo. Remember, for legal (copyright and trademark) reasons, your logo cannot look like any other logo. You'll find skilled and experienced graphic designers you can hire on services like UpWork.com. Be sure to check out the webpages, social media accounts, and gaming channels from some of your favorite YouTubers and online personalities to see how they've utilized a logo to help brand and customize their online content.

Choose Your Streaming Service

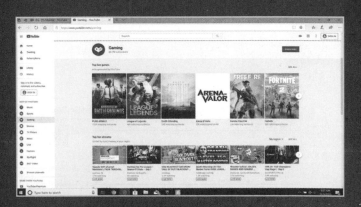

The majority of online personalities who specialize in pre-recorded videos make their online home on YouTube—the world's largest and most popular video streaming service.

Those who choose to stream live typically must choose which streaming service they want to focus on, so they're able to build up their audience on one main platform. If you choose to publish videos on YouTube, and then stream randomly on YouTube Live, Twitch, and/or Mixer, while making recordings of your live streams available on-demand on multiple services as well, you'll quickly confuse your audience because they won't know when and where to easily find you and your latest content.

Especially if you're a new and up-and-coming content creator, focus on posting your videos or hosting your live streams on just one service. Choose a service that caters well to the *Fortnite* community, that is popular among the people in your target audience, and that offers the tools and resources that'll allow you to create and publish/broadcast the content you want, in the easiest and most professional way possible.

How to Establish Yourself on Twitch

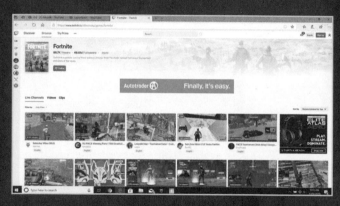

Twitch is a free online service dedicated to gamers. It's a place on the Internet where literally millions of people from all over the world congregate every day to chat, interact, and make their own entertainment by hosting or watching live streams. While Twitch offers separate areas for music, talk shows, sports, special events, and other topic-specific content, it has become one of the Internet's largest online communities for live streams related to gaming, including Fortnite: Battle Royale.

At any given moment—anytime day or night—more than 1.3 million people are online watching Twitch live streams. During a typical day, this equates to more than 15 million people visiting the service. Each month, more than three million content creators host live steams. Tens of thousands of those Twitch creators qualify to join the Twitch Partner Program and ultimately are able to earn some money from their efforts and online exploits.

Before you start streaming live on Twitch, set up a free Twitch account by visiting www.twitch.tv and clicking on the Sign Up button that's located in the top-right corner of the browser window. If you're using a smartphone or tablet, be sure to download and install the official Twitch app onto your iPhone, iPad, or Android-based mobile device. You can then set up a free Twitch account from within the mobile app.

Next, take the time to watch a handful of already successful Twitch streamers—especially those who focus on gaming and Fortnite content. Discover what's expected of you and what's possible during live streams.

If you think you might want to become a Twitch streamer, access the Twitch Creator Camp (www.twitch.tv/creatorcamp/en) and learn all about what's involved, while obtaining step-by-step directions for establishing and hosting a successful broadcast. Begin by clicking on the Get Started button.

To stream on Twitch, you'll need the right equipment, a reliable high-speed Internet connection, as well as an active Twitch account. The equipment you'll need will vary, based on whether you want to broadcast from a computer, PlayStation 4, or Xbox One, for example. As a console-based gamer, if you want to simultaneously broadcast your live gaming stream and show your face, for example, this will require additional equipment.

When using a computer to stream, you'll likely want to use the free Twitch Studio software (https://help.twitch.tv/s/article/twitch-studio-faq). This is an all-in-one streaming app that's ideal for beginners. As you grow your channel and require more advanced functionality, third-party software can be used to make your live streams look even more professional.

Especially if you want to stream live gaming content, in conjunction with yourself, you'll need specialized broadcasting software for your Windows PC or Mac. There are more than a dozen third-party software options you can use, such as OBS Project, Xsplit, XSplit Gamecaster, Shameshow Live, Bebo, Wirecast, Vmix, Eigato Game Capture, Live Gamer Extreme, and Light Stream.

XPlit GameCaster (www.xsplit.com/gamecaster), for example, is free Windows PC software that's compatible with Twitch, Mixer, Facebook, and YouTube. It's designed to make game-related live streams easy. The Premium edition of this software is priced at $149.95 for a three-year unlimited subscription, although less expensive and shorter term subscriptions are available. To learn how to use this software, access the XSplit Academy online (www.xsplit.com/academy). This is just one example of software you can use to manage and produce your own live streams.

To learn more about the third-party applications that work with Twitch (and often other live streaming services), visit: https://help.twitch.tv/s/article/recommended-software-for-broadcasting.

As you're establishing your channel, you'll definitely want to customize and personalize it. This is called "branding." One of the ways you can customize your channel, plus add more functionality to it, is to utilize free Extensions (www.twitch.tv/p/extensions).

The first section of Twitch Creator Camp is called Learn the Basics. This area teaches you how to build your channel, gather and set up the equipment you'll need, and then walks you through the process of hosting your very first live stream.

As a Twitch streamer, you'll eventually be able to expand your channel and build your relationship with the Twitch service. When you first get started, you're classified simply as a "Streamer." Anyone can become a streamer for free.

Once you reach Affiliate status on Twitch (https://affiliate.twitch.tv), your channel will automatically receive a Subscribe button, so your online friends and followers can support you and your channel by paying a small monthly fee to receive bonus content. At this point, you'll have the ability to earn money from your broadcasts.

However, only after you've achieved several more specific milestones during your live streams (for example, you've broadcasted for more than 25 hours, you've had broadcasts on at least 12 unique days within the last 30 days, and your audience has included at least 75 viewers per stream), will you qualify to become a Twitch Partner (www.twitch.tv/p/partners).

Twitch Partnership allows you to earn more revenue in more ways in conjunction with your live streams. For example, in addition to earning money from Subscriptions, you'll receive ad revenue based on viewers seeing ads which are displayed on your channel page and potentially before and during your live streams.

Be sure to visit the Twitch 101 web page to learn more about the differences between being a Streamer, Affiliate, and Partner (www.twitch.tv/creatorcamp/en/learn-the-basics/twitch-101).

Start Streaming on Mixer

Owned and operated by Microsoft, Mixer (formally known as Beam) is another extremely popular online gaming community that allows hobbyists and professionals alike to stream gaming content live. It's also the exclusive online home for Ninja's live Fortnite streams (https://mixer.com/Ninja), although at any given time, you'll discover hundreds of gamers streaming Fortnite-related content. Keep in mind, Mixer supports all gaming platforms, not just Windows PCs and the Xbox One.

Once you decide to join Mixer as a streamer, you'll want to visit https://mixer.com/dashboard/onboarding, and click on the Get Started Now button to set up your account and establish your channel. Mixer also requires that you have an active Microsoft account (https://account.microsoft.com/account), whether you're a viewer, Hobbyist streamer, or Mixer Partner. Next, spend some time learning about this streaming platform by participating in the online tutorials offered by Mixer Academy (https://academy.mixer.com/en-us).

Anyone can start streaming as a Hobbyist anytime, but if you want to upgrade your channel to become a Mixer Partner and earn revenue from your streaming efforts, you'll need to apply for this status after meeting the following qualifications:

- **Your Mixer account must be at least 2 months old**
- **You must have at least 2,000 followers**
- **You must stream at least 12 unique days per month**
- **You must stream at least 25 hours per month**

Like Twitch, you can use any of several different Windows or Mac applications to stream live on Mixer. Streams can be done directly from an Xbox One with no additional software. However, to stream using a computer or another console-based system, one of the free, open source applications for this purpose is called OBS Studio (https://obsproject.com). XSplit (www.xsplit.com/#broadcaster) is another free application that's commonly used for streaming on Mixer and similar services.

Establish Your Own YouTube Channel or Broadcast Live on YouTube

In addition to offering the world's largest collection of pre-recorded, on-demand video content —including thousands of hours' worth of *Fortnite*-related content from Epic Games (www.youtube.com/user/epicfortnite) and independent content creators, YouTube offers the ability to broadcast live via its YouTube Live service.

Anyone who wants to create and showcase content on YouTube needs to create their own YouTube channel. It's then possible to customize the channel with a unique name, URL, logo, and other content. You're also able to organize and showcase your videos and playlists in a variety ways.

Once you decide to launch your own YouTube channel, head over to the online-based YouTube Creator Academy (https://creatoracademy.youtube.com) for a comprehensive guide on how to get started, manage and grow your channel, and eventually earn money from your channel and/or live streams.

After committing to creating *Fortnite*-related videos to be published on YouTube, you need to begin creating content on a regular basis that offers production quality that's equal to or superior to the other YouTubers also publishing gaming content on this platform. This will require you to utilize a good-quality camera, lighting, microphone, some type of backdrop, and pro-level editing techniques. Thus, you'll need to develop basic video production and editing skills, on top of becoming a highly skilled gamer.

In addition to traditional gaming videos—where viewers watch you play *Fortnite* in a pre-recorded video or a live stream, there are many different ways of creating compelling content that's *Fortnite* related. For example, you could share tips and tutorials, offer first impressions (reactions) related to game updates, create videos featuring competitions between you and specific other gamers, showcase *Fortnite: Creative* maps you've created, or show yourself experiencing other people's *Fortnite: Creative* maps or Deathruns.

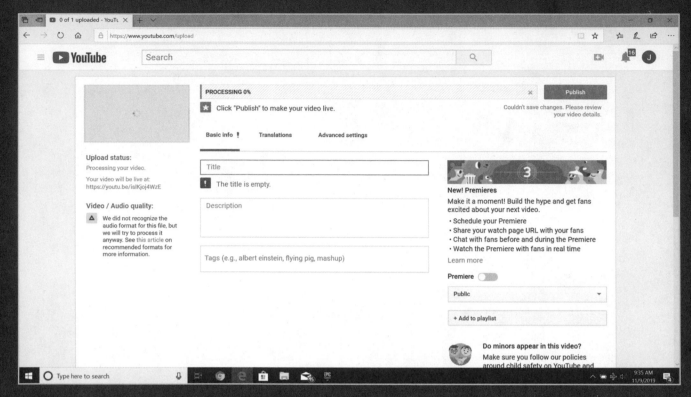

Beyond offering top-notch production quality as well as informative or entertaining content that's original and creative, one of the most important aspects of publishing YouTube content on your channel is learning how to create catchy video titles and descriptions that'll capture the attention of perspective viewers and encourage your subscribers to watch new videos right away.

It's also important that all content on your channel be related. For example, if the main focus of your channel is showcasing *Fortnite* game tips and tutorials, don't randomly add videos about other games or unrelated topics. Consistency in your content and a regular publishing schedule for new videos is important for maintaining and growing your audience.

Since interaction with your YouTube audience is so important, you'll definitely want to encourage your viewers to "like," comment, and share each of your videos, and subscribe to your YouTube channel.

Get Started Using Facebook Watch

Just about everyone knows that Facebook is the world's most popular social media platform with more than two billion active users. In addition to maintaining a Facebook page that can be used to promote your YouTube videos or live streams on other platforms, the Facebook service offers Facebook Watch (www.facebook.com/watch), which is similar to YouTube in that it offers a place to publish pre-recorded, on-demand videos.

To begin publishing videos that become accessible on Facebook Watch (in addition to your own Facebook page), your Facebook page must have at least 5,000 followers, or you must have a verified Facebook profile with at least 50,000 followers. However, anyone can publish on-demand videos as part of their own Facebook page.

From your Facebook page, it's also possible to broadcast live (using the Facebook Live tools). This can include live game streams. To learn more about broadcasting live from your Facebook page, visit: www.facebook.com/help/publisher/167417030499767?id=383172118863825.

To create your own Facebook page, start by pointing your web browser to: www.facebook.com/pages/creation.

As a gamer, select the Get Started button associated with the Community or Public Figure option. Next, create an original and attention-grabbing Page Name, and choose a category for your Facebook page. The category you select might be Gaming Video Creator, Video Game, or Gamer.

Until you reach the level where your videos are published on Facebook Watch, consider publishing your pre-recorded, on-demand videos on your own YouTube channel as well, and simply using Facebook as a way to promote that YouTube channel and to interact with your audience.

SECTION 6

FORTNITE: BATTLE ROYALE
ONLINE RESOURCES

From this unofficial guide, hopefully you've discovered that becoming a "pro" *Fortnite* gamer can mean a lot of different things. For some, it means winning tournaments and competitions and becoming a top-ranked player. For others, it means launching a YouTube channel that focuses on some aspect of *Fortnite*, or perhaps becoming a live streamer on a service like Twitch or Mixer.

This section offers a bunch of online resources that you'll find useful when it comes to enhancing your gaming skills and staying up to date on everything having to do with *Fortnite*. Of course, you'll also want to start watching the YouTube videos and live streams from some of the most popular *Fortnite* gamers to round out or expand your *Fortnite* gaming knowledge.

WEBSITE OR YOUTUBE CHANNEL NAME	DESCRIPTION	URL
All-Stars eSports League	An online service that hosts online and site-based *Fortnite* competitions and tournaments specifically for high schoolers.	www.allstaresports.com
Astro Gaming	A company that manufactures and sells pro-level controllers for computers and console-based systems.	www.astrogaming.com
Best *Fortnite* Settings	Discover the custom game settings used by some of the world's top-rated *Fortnite: Battle Royale* players.	www.bestfortnitesettings.com
Checkmate Gaming Network	An online service that hosts online-based *Fortnite* competitions and tournaments.	www.checkmategaming.com
CoachingGames.net	One of the online services that allows you to hire "professional" *Fortnite* game coaches.	https://coaching-games.net /coaching/fortnite-coaching
Corsair	Consider upgrading your keyboard and mouse to equipment that's designed specifically for gaming. Corsair is one of several companies that manufactures keyboards, mice, and headsets specifically for gamers.	www.corsair.com
Discord's *Fortnite* Forum	Visit this popular, online-based discussion group that has almost 400,000 members.	https://discordapp.com /invite/fortnite
Epic Game's Official Social Media Accounts for *Fortnite*	Visit the official Facebook, Twitter, and Instagram Accounts for *Fortnite*. Be sure to use the **#Fortnite** hashtag to find specific Twitter discussions and Instagram posts covering the game.	Facebook: www.facebook.com/FortniteGame Twitter: https://twitter.com/fortnitegame Instagram: www.instagram.com/fortnite

WEBSITE OR YOUTUBE CHANNEL NAME	DESCRIPTION	URL
Fandom's *Fortnite* Wiki	Discover the latest news and strategies related to *Fortnite*.	http://fortnite.wikia.com /wiki/Fortnite_Wiki
FBR Insider	The *Fortnite: Battle Royale Insider* website offers game-related news, tips, and strategy videos.	www.fortniteinsider.com
Fortnite Creative HQ	An independent online resource that showcases more than 3,000 Creative maps. Check out the Featured and Trending sections of the website to discover the very best maps.	www.fortnitecreativehq.com
Fortnite Gamepedia Wiki	Read up-to-date descriptions of every weapon, loot item, and ammo type available within *Fortnite*. This Wiki also maintains a comprehensive database of soldier outfits and related items released by Epic Games.	https://fortnite.gamepedia. com/Fortnite_Wiki For Mission-related information, visit: https: //fortnite.gamepedia.com /Missions
Fortnite Scout	Check your personal player stats, and analyze your performance using a bunch of colorful graphs and charts. Also check out the stats of other *Fortnite: Battle Royale* players.	www.fortnitescout.com
Fortnite Skins	This independent website maintains a detailed database of all *Fortnite: Battle Royale* outfits and accessory items released by Epic Games.	https://fortniteskins.net
Fortnite Stats	An independent website that allows you to track the rankings for almost any *Fortnite* player.	https://fortnitestats.net
Fortnite Tracker Network	A website that showcases many Creative Maps and provides gamers with the codes to access them.	https://fortnitetracker.com /creative
Fortnite Weapon Stats & Info	This website offers up-to-date information on all of the weapons currently available in *Fortnite: Battle Royale*.	https://fortnitestats.com /weapons
Fortnite: Battle Royale for Android Mobile Devices	Download *Fortnite: Battle Royale* for your compatible Android-based mobile device.	www.epicgames.com /fortnite/en-US/mobile /android/get-started

WEBSITE OR YOUTUBE CHANNEL NAME	DESCRIPTION	URL
Fortnite: Battle Royale Mobile (iOS App Store)	Download *Fortnite: Battle Royale* for your Apple iPhone or iPad	https://itunes.apple.com/us/app/fortnite/id1261357853
Fortnitebase.net	Access Leaderboards for *Fortnite* and keep tabs on the top ranked players.	https://fortbase.net/leadboards
Game Informer Magazine's *Fortnite* Coverage	Discover articles, reviews, and news about *Fortnite* published by *Game Informer* magazine.	www.gameinformer.com/fortnite
Gamepedia *Fortnite* Wiki	This website offers up-to-date information about all of the weapons, items, outfits, etc., that are currently available in *Fortnite: Battle Royale*.	https://fortnite.gamepedia.com/Fortnite_Wiki
GamerzArena	An online service that hosts online-based *Fortnite* competitions and tournaments.	www.gamerzarena.com
GameSpot's *Fortnite* Coverage	Check out the news, reviews, and game coverage related to *Fortnite* that's been published by GameSpot.	www.gamespot.com/fortnite
GamingCoach.gg	One of the online services that allows you to hire "professional" *Fortnite* game coaches.	https://gamingcoach.gg/game/fortnite
HyperX Gaming	Manufactures a selection of high-quality gaming keyboards, mice, headsets, and other accessories used by amateur and pro gamers alike. These work on PCs, Macs, and most console-based gaming systems.	www.hyperxgaming.com
IGN Fortnite Wiki Guide	Check out all IGN's past and current coverage of *Fortnite*.	www.ign.com/wikis/fortnite
Jason R. Rich's Websites and Social Media	Learn about additional, unofficial game strategy guides by Jason R. Rich that cover *Fortnite*, *PUBG*, *Brawl Stars*, *Overwatch*, and *Apex Legends* (each sold separately).	www.JasonRich.com www.GameTipBooks.com Twitter: @JasonRich7 Instagram: @JasonRich7
Kyle Giersdorf (also known as "Bugha")	Winner of the 2019 *Fortnite* World Cup	YouTube: www.youtube.com/channel/UCgIoEgOk3wzhhORNC9AbzhQ Twitch.tv: www.twitch.tv/bugha

WEBSITE OR YOUTUBE CHANNEL NAME	DESCRIPTION	URL
LazarBeam	With around 12 million subscribers, LazarBeam offers *Fortnite* tutorials that are not only informative, but very funny and extremely entertaining. You'll definitely want to subscribe to his YouTube channel!	YouTube Channel www.youtube.com /Lazarbeam Twitter: https://twitter.com /LazarBeamYT Instagram: www.instagram. com/lazarbeamyt
Logitech	An independent company that manufactures pro-level gaming keyboards, mice, and other hardware.	www.logitech.com
Microsoft's Xbox One *Fortnite* Website	Learn about and acquire *Fortnite: Battle Royale* if you're an Xbox One gamer.	www.microsoft.com/en-US /store/p/Fortnite-Battle -Royalee/BT5P2X999VH2
Mixer	An online gaming service for streaming live gaming content.	www.mixer.com
Nacon Gaming	A company that manufactures and sells pro-level controllers for computers and console-based systems.	www.nacongaming.com
Ninja	Check out the live and recorded game streams from Ninja, one of the most highly skilled *Fortnite: Battle Royale* players in the world. His YouTube channel, for example, has more than 22 million subscribers.	YouTube: www.youtube.com /user/NinjasHyper Mixer: www.mixer.com/ninja
Official Epic Games YouTube Channel for *Fortnite: Battle Royale*	The official *Fortnite: Battle Royale* YouTube channel.	www.youtube.com/user /epicfortnite
ProGuides	One of the online services that allows you to hire "professional" *Fortnite* game coaches.	www.proguides.com
Razer	A company that offers high-end gaming controllers, keyboards, mice, and gaming headsets designed for more advanced gamers.	www.razer.com
Reddit's *Fortnite: Creative* Forum	Join thousands of *Fortnite* enthusiasts in an ongoing discussion that includes gaming tips and strategies.	www.reddit.com/r/Fortnite www.reddit.com/r/ FortNiteBR
Roccat Gaming	An independent company that manufactures pro-level gaming keyboards, mice, and other hardware.	https://en.roccat.org

WEBSITE OR YOUTUBE CHANNEL NAME	DESCRIPTION	URL
SCUF Gaming	This company makes high-end, extremely precise, customizable controllers for the console-based gaming systems, including the SCUF Impact controller for the PS4. If you're looking to enhance your reaction times when playing *Fortnite*, consider upgrading your wireless or wired controller.	www.scufgaming.com
SteelSeries	An independent company that manufactures pro-level gaming keyboards, mice, and other hardware.	https://steelseries.com
The Players' Lounge	An online service that hosts online-based *Fortnite* competitions and tournaments.	https://playerslounge.co /games
Turtle Beach Corp.	This is one of many companies that make great quality, wired or wireless (Bluetooth) gaming headsets that work with all gaming platforms.	www.turtlebeach.com
Twitch.tv	An online gaming service for streaming live gaming content.	www.twitch.tv

Fortnite Is Not Just a Game . . . Playing Could Become Your Job!

Throughout the year, Epic Games, along with a wide range of independent companies, hosts *Fortnite: Battle Royale* tournaments, content, and challenges where the winners and top-ranked players can take home thousands of dollars (and in some cases millions of dollars) in prize money.

If you already have what it takes to become a pro player and take home some of this cash, congratulations! However, if you're like most of us, reaching pro status in *Fortnite: Battle Royale* will first require you to master a bunch of game-related skills, and then invest countless hours practicing.

No matter how good you get playing *Fortnite: Battle Royale*, thanks to the continuous upgrades and patches that Epic Games releases, the game continues to evolve, which means that with each new gaming season, there will always be new things to discover and new challenges to overcome.

Even if you don't win the *Fortnite World Cup*, perhaps you could tap your gaming skills and experience to become a professional *Fortnite* coach and make money helping other gamers improve their skills.

Meanwhile, just about anyone with a passion for gaming can become a YouTuber or live streamer and share their skills, knowledge, and love for *Fortnite* with a potentially global audience. And if you become popular online, there's plenty of opportunity to earn money from your efforts.

The focus of this unofficial guide was on how to take your gaming to the next level, with the goal of potentially becoming a pro. The other books in this *Master Combat Series* by Jason R. Rich focus on helping you improve your gaming skills by featuring tips and strategies for experiencing specific aspects of *Fortnite*, whether it's *Fortnite: Battle Royale, Fortnite:*

Save the World, or *Fortnite: Creative*, so be sure to check out these other information-packed guides. To learn more about them, visit www. FortniteGameBooks.com.

Whatever you do, remember that *Fortnite: Battle Royale* is a game. It's designed to be fun and challenging to play. However much you push yourself as a gamer to continuously improve your gaming skills, don't forget to have fun playing!